Psychoanalysis, Culture and Contemporary Discontents

Ricardo Rubinstein explores the contemporary culture and its discontents – including subjectivity, fanaticism, panic attacks, technology, and pandemics – through a psychoanalytic lens.

Each chapter considers an aspect of modern society and attempts to unpick these complex facets of the world we live in. Psychoanalytic understandings of the triggers and socio-environmental factors of panic attacks, the inner worlds of people attracted to fanatical beliefs and risky behaviours, and our dependence on technology for our most vital activities are explored in an accessible way. Rubinstein also considers the restrictions put in place on the lives of millions of people as a result of the COVID-19 pandemic and examines human adaptation to restrictive conditions. *Psychoanalysis, Culture and Contemporary Discontents* is illustrated throughout with clinical vignettes from the author's practice.

This psychoanalytic exploration of a diverse range of topical issues will be of interest to psychoanalysts and psychoanalytic psychotherapists in practice and in training. It will also be relevant for academics and students of sociology and cultural studies and to readers interested in understanding cultural concerns in more depth.

Ricardo Alejandro Rubinstein is a doctor, psychiatrist, training psychoanalyst of the Argentine Psychoanalytic Association, and full member of the International Psychoanalytical Association. He has also been a Professor at the Center of Psychoanalytical Teaching. He is the author of *Sports on the Couch* (Routledge, 2017), which is also available in Spanish and Romanian.

Psychoanalysis, Culture and Contemporary Discontents

A Time of Technology, Fanaticism and Pandemics

Ricardo Alejandro Rubinstein

Routledge
Taylor & Francis Group
LONDON AND NEW YORK

Cover image: © Boris SV/Getty Images

First published 2023
by Routledge
4 Park Square, Milton Park, Abingdon, Oxon OX14 4RN

and by Routledge
605 Third Avenue, New York, NY 10158

Routledge is an imprint of the Taylor & Francis Group, an informa business

© 2023 Ricardo Alejandro Rubinstein

British Library Cataloguing-in-Publication Data
A catalogue record for this book is available from the British Library

Library of Congress Cataloging-in-Publication Data
A catalog record has been requested for this book

ISBN: 978-1-032-27633-5 (hbk)
ISBN: 978-1-032-27632-8 (pbk)
ISBN: 978-1-003-29356-9 (ebk)

DOI: 10.4324/9781003293569

Typeset in Times New Roman
by KnowledgeWorks Global Ltd.

To Nico, Juli, Mora, Ciro, and Isabella,
my grandsons

Contents

Foreword

Buenos Aires, August 2021. Full coronavirus pandemic. Less than 30% of the population is fully vaccinated. Waiting for a new wave due to the circulation of the Delta variant, which is sweeping the Northern hemisphere. The country is going through a serious economic crisis, with more than 40% of poverty and 50% of children in poverty. There are few expectations about the upcoming elections, although politicians are fighting for their possible positions. The world is on edge because of the US withdrawal from Afghanistan and the advance of the Taliban regime, with the martyrdom of women that this implies. But it is powerless.

All this is just a click away in our computers or phones when in the past we used to hear about it in the next day newspapers or on the TV news, and, long ago, several weeks or months after the events. Even for those of us who are not digital natives, it is very easy to access this information, although we run the risk of being over-informed or selectively informed, moved by algorithms that detect our possible interests. On the other hand, for the children of this era, contact with screens from a very early age cannot be without consequences in their psychic structuring in their subjective constitution. We know more and more about the potential beneficial and harmful effects of this digital immersion through screens at a time of life when the psyche and subjectivity are being generated.

Childhood vulnerability or helplessness, which persists in different ways in adulthood, exposes children to harmful influences, often disruptive and potentially traumatic, especially in the face of a stimulus overload and the lack of protective barriers. Deficits in parental functions do not escape this state of affairs and give rise to undesirable outcomes.

In this context, which enhances vulnerability, it is not surprising that there are states of anguish that we now characterize as panic crises or that there is a search for unloading mechanisms or self-soothing procedures in risk sports or in the increase of fanaticism. These are the topics that the interesting and entertaining book we have in our hands deals with in depth.

Although we know that psychoanalysts cannot be oblivious to the culture of the time and the society in which they live, it is not frequent to find perspectives that articulate this knowledge as we see in this work. The borders between disciplines delimit epistemologies and discourses, but they should not fragment the reality I tried to describe in the opening paragraphs.

Psychoanalytic training requires knowledge of this type of scenarios, and any reader interested in these issues has in psychoanalysis a source of knowledge that is enriched when it is articulated with the contributions of other disciplines. A book that introduces us to these issues is always welcome.

Although this book has been written by a psychoanalyst, it is crossed by interdisciplinary contributions that show an open psychoanalysis and a restless psychoanalyst who takes us through well-updated paths of different disciplines trying to account for the world we live in. The contributions of biology, physiology, sociology, literature, communication theory, linguistics, philosophy, chaos theories, among others, are part of this intertwining.

Studying panic attack, the eroticization of danger, fanaticism, the impact of technology, and now of the pandemic is important for a psychoanalyst and of interest to any curious general reader. Besides, the clinical exemplification, always welcome, allows us to enter into the author's clinical work.

In the case of panic attack, it is a condition of increasing prevalence that challenges all health care workers – not only in the field of mental health. These situations are frequently seen in hospital wards; the sensation of imminent death requires a quick differential diagnosis, especially in the case of coronary episodes. They also require an approach combining psychotherapy and psychopharmacology, and psychoanalysis offers theoretical tools for this type of intervention, provided that the uniqueness of each patient is not lost, even if the psychopathogenic mechanism is the same for all.

For its part, the pandemic forces us to weigh the hypercomplexity of current circumstances. A paradigmatic example is the impact on our lives of the digital world and the necessary handling of technology that it implies.

Julio Campos describes three current threats: the virus, the restriction posed by the quarantine, and the subjugation to the digital we are experiencing. To paraphrase Ortega y Gasset, being digitally uninformed or ignorant implies not understanding computers and their "circumstances". These are, as Claudio Eizirik describes, unmapped territories, unknown to most of us but very accessible to the new generations.

In this sense, I do not believe in the usefulness of exclusively intradisciplinary debates. I think that psychoanalysis, far from pretending to be a *Weltanschauung*, must take into account this hypercomplexity by including itself in a transdisciplinary perspective.

Flavia Costa describes the current epoch as the "Technocene", characterized by hypercomplexity and by a very rapid technological change, which entails a very high risk and will leave traces in us and in several future generations. This is in addition to an exaggerated growth of the Bios, with an uneven distribution of wealth. In this context, for this author, it is a matter of reducing the risks of what Perrow called "normal or systemic accidents", which are inevitable but foreseeable. That is why we must be able to think these things through. They are just examples of the necessary interdisciplinary attitude to adopt in our debates.

I think that psychoanalysis will grow at the interfaces with the rest of the cultural realms in which we practice it, that it will go beyond its limits or boundaries, and that circumstances like these especially challenge prejudices about moving away from "caricatures" and the "typical cure", and allow us to explore uncharted territory.

With this in mind, the International Psychoanalytic Association (IPA) is developing programs such as "IPA in the community" and "IPA in the world", which attempt to account for the contexts in which contemporary psychoanalysis is developing.

Starting from the clinical work in its different modalities, the topics examined here are fanaticism, prejudice, violence, discrimination (especially racism), education, politics in the world, among others.

I hope that this brief introduction will serve as a stimulus to delve into these pages. I personally know the author and am well-aware of his wide-ranging interests. To be presented in English and in a prestigious collection will bring him closer to readers in many countries.

If we think with Pontalis that psychoanalysis is an essentially migratory discipline, moving from one language or dialect to another, from one culture to another, from one kind of knowledge to another, we will agree with him that learning to migrate, the experience of doing so, stimulates reflection and learning. In this migratory capacity, in the tolerance to the encounter with the other, in doubt and uncertainty, lies the heart of the analytical experience.

The reading of these pages constitutes an invitation to carry out that task and their dissemination in other languages and cultures will enhance that migration between theories or disciplines to which the author invites us.

Dr Abel Mario Fainstein
Former President of Argentine Psychoanalytic Association (APA), and
Former President of Latin American Psychoanalytic Federation (FEPAL)

Introduction

The present time in which we live is crossed by circumstances and experiences that generate commotion and deep impacts on subjectivity; at the same time, they agglutinate and spread effects at a planetary level, as never happened before.

The environment that surrounds us, our cultures and global communications make it possible to homogenize many of the ways in which these effects manifest and externalize themselves so as to place them under the magnifying glass of our psychoanalytic reflection.

This does not occur in a humanistic context such as that of the end of the 19th century, when psychoanalysis emerged, nor even in a context of ideals of perfection and improvement in the Hellenic manner. In this postmodern era, the set of values, symbols, traditions, beliefs, and forms of behaviour (habits, customs) that we dynamically share today with almost the entire world, together with universalized languages, integrate us and make us share the same codes, expectations, and sufferings.

We are living in an era of omnipresent images and are submerged, immersed, harassed, and accompanied by them. These images are easier to generate than verbal discourses, which they threaten to displace mercilessly, intruding both in the public sphere and (in an increasingly blatant way) in the private sphere.

The previous culture of modernism, teleologically and metaphysically driven by progress and perfection, a culture of repression, of the sublimation of instincts, of discontent, and guilt, gradually gave way to a broad repertoire of cultural manifestations with new forms of discontent.

Although the mechanism of repression as a source of subjective discomfort has not lost its validity, other expressions have gained a place today: the sensation of emptiness, the banality of behaviour in the public space, the dilution of ethical values as regulators of behaviour, with a predominance of aesthetic values (linked to images), the permanent dissatisfaction conducive to excessive consumption, the place of material reality, overwhelmed by virtual reality.

DOI: 10.4324/9781003293569-1

Individuals tend to feel increasingly cornered by the environment and the machines. Their critical capacity, the one that enables them to appropriate the subjective aspect of experience, is checked and diluted in their effective capacity to act in the public sphere, while their sense of self is more and more imprisoned and relegated.

Culture has always been imbued with a discontent inherent to the constitution of the subject: the death drive. This happened throughout history, but humans found the means to contain or tame the aggressive and destructive instincts and impulses that they harboured within themselves. They were able to compensate for the instinctive renunciations through libidinal bonds and satisfactions provided by social and communitarian ideals that gave them a sense of participation and belonging, recognition, security, and shelter. Integration in a social group acts as a narcissistic support and offers the subject a base that allows him to feel stability. If we consider this environment as a whole as a containing social membrane that allows us to identify ourselves, constitute ourselves and be in the world – a sort of social envelope of the self – , we observe that when it is altered, it seriously affects not only the constitution of these membranes but also the individual psychic envelopes and structures of each subject. The absence of a social environment that provides links for the libido facilitates the latter's regression to the Ego. In such circumstances, not being able to concretize a creative action that provides an intersubjective pulsional driven channel, since this option is suppressed, a possible destiny is to acquire power over others, which exacerbates loneliness and individualism and abolishes social supports. Aggression as a form of connection with the other is installed as a valid alternative and leads to the terrain of violence. In this instance, the denial of the selfhood of others is also the denial of one's own self.

We see these symptoms starkly in fanaticism (which we discuss in depth in this book), just as in another way we observe it in screen addicts. In both cases, the denial of the subject as a fellow human being, as a human other, shows its sinister and silent deadly facet.

At present, a conjunction of factors has altered both in quality and quantity the conformation of interpersonal bonds, with consequences at the social and individual levels. The common denominator of this is subjective discomfort and suffering. Enrique Pichon Rivière stated that "behind every sick behavior there is also a social conflict; the main morbid factor is the social one".

The discourse of globalization (which aims at the supposed disappearance of differences and frontiers between countries and cultures by establishing an illusory single possible world), together with the increase in technological progress and the predominance of market rules over other values, led to the shaking of myths and beliefs rooted for generations, as well as to a violent clash between civilizations, opposing fundamentalisms and protective nationalisms to divergent uniformity. At the same time, the death of God, the end of history, and the fall of political ideologies and religious beliefs added to the insecurity and confusion of vast human groups.

Another factor is the possibility of access to paid work and socioeconomic well-being. Uncertainty, instability, and unemployment bring with them economic urgencies. As a result, it is not possible to generate a creative bonding for the libido and social dispersion movements are generated, as well as processes of vulnerability and subjective and bonding fragmentation. The great migrations caused by wars, natural catastrophes, and, more recently, pandemics have been crucial in this regard.

The inner space of the family, as a traditional institution, has undergone substantial changes in parallel to the crises of the State and religion. The change in relations between the sexes, especially as regards the social status of women, led to a transformation of the dynamics of relationships, codes of exchange, and authority structures.

The increase in divorce and single-parent families, the restricted periods of cohabitation with relatives, and the lower incidence of parental protection deteriorated the patterns of child-rearing, together with the increase in child abuse due to neglect or domestic violence. These aspects, highlighted by demographers, lead to an increase in aggressive tendencies inside and outside the home and, on a large scale, pave the way for a violent society. Likewise, the decreasing amount of time devoted to daily activities shared in recreational spaces and to emotional exchanges (which only take place during family gatherings, such as meals and weekends) has now been swallowed up by the absorption with screens.

This set of causes, responsible for social stress, with crises that become more acute from time to time, undermine the narcissistic support base provided by the environment, which gives stability to the subjects. They expose the inconsistencies of being and are responsible for breaks and discontinuities that imply a rupture of our daily life, with experiences of uncertainty for the future, chaos, helplessness, as well as the increase of frustrations and hardships. The social and the individual intertwine giving rise to intense states of discomfort, pathogenic symptoms, and processes of psychic suffering. Such subjective suffering is thus the product of the inability to preserve and sustain over time a trophic narcissistic social, family, and subjective organization capable of containing and accompanying the internal processes of growth, exchange, and transformation necessary for psychosocial development.

It is important that the convergence of fields of approach, study, and observation of these phenomena allow the joint construction of spaces and objects of knowledge, taking care not to blur the boundaries of each discipline. Psychoanalysis can expand by attempting a complementary interaction and opening new perspectives on such phenomena in order to shed light on them. To this end, it is necessary to understand the epistemic differences, conceptual categories, and diverse modes of semantic expression of each field of knowledge. The social, economic, demographic, or anthropological concepts provided by different approaches should not make us lose sight of the appreciation of subjective suffering linked to the unconscious motivations of behaviour.

It is very noticeable that the tremendous sociocultural exigencies, with their pressing times and overadaptive demands, very actively reinforce the pathologies we see today. Structuring functional failures, both paternal and maternal, generated by stressful socioenvironmental changes (single-parent families, work, migrations) acutely promote the appearance of very demanding ideals, which function as a reactive compensation for these failures and give rise to a pathology of ideals, with projective forms placed in external reality.

Its functioning generates a paradoxical situation since the subject deposits its problems in the outside, as we see in those who eroticize danger and seek experiences and adventures in Nature with an enlivening effect. All this turns back on the subject himself, often in the form of somatic illnesses or heroic efforts that result in injuries and accidents. It is an evident example of the repercussion of the social on bodies and minds.

This collection of facts and factors, each with their own codes, provoke the resurgence of old pathologies in current clothes. It can be observed in panic attacks and fanaticism in its various manifestations, as well as in the appearance of other conditions associated with the same suffering – which is none other than anguish, helplessness, powerlessness, unhappiness, misery, and hopelessness in their current forms, with their sequel of limitations.

In a comprehensive vision, we could say that we are affected by three major types of disorders: (1) Those related to the current lifestyle. (2) The new addictions to objects and behaviours. (3) Disorders related to self-image.

In the first group, we place the effects of maladaptation to the environment and its demands, generating states of stress, anguish, and panic, as well as loneliness and feelings of inadequacy and emptiness.

In the second group are the effects produced by the search for actions or objects used to reduce tensions and achieve stimulating biochemical effects without exogenous drugs. Subjects become dependent and addicted in order to evade their painful reality. They feel an irrepressible impulse, a sensation of pleasure and well-being while performing these activities, which lead them to isolate themselves from their surroundings and generate a state of altered consciousness; if they do not perform them, they suffer a withdrawal syndrome. In both cases, the consequence is a significant family, social, occupational, and economic breakdown.

In many of these situations, anonymity favours disinhibition. Dependence on certain objects is an increasingly widespread behaviour. The individual feels better and more secure by possessing certain things. This can be observed in those who eroticize danger and in screen addicts, who turn their painful, distressing, and unhappy feelings into feelings of strength and power.

In the third group, we find disorders related to self-image. These are people obsessed with health, beauty, and perfection, whose ideals are largely promoted by the mass media. In the age of image, these disorders are becoming more and more frequent. Anorexia, bulimia, bigorexia, polysurgeries that change and retouch various parts of the body, addiction to certain styles of eating, etc.

Of all the new possible clinical pictures, I decided to investigate in depth only some of them in the following chapters. They have a common basis and some particularities that we will see below.

Panic attack; the eroticization of danger, adventure, and adrenalin; fanaticism; the addictive tendencies generated by new technologies; the psychic consequences of the COVID-19 pandemic: these are the ailments of our time with a high impact on enormous masses of the population. They recognize a similar origin and contexts that propitiate their appearance. In all these cases, there is an increase in the vulnerability of the subjects, product of disruptive, harmful and traumatic influences, which lead to an overload of stimuli, an overflow of social and family protection barriers, which translates into varying degrees of psychic suffering and affects bodies, minds, and ways of acting.

Panic is a condition whose incidence has grown enormously in recent years and has been further enhanced during the pandemic, to the point that more than a third of the world's population has been actually or potentially affected by its symptoms. They invalidate and tremendously affect the work capacity of the subjects and compromise the family and social life due to the limitations it entails in daily life, movement and transportation, or to loneliness or the permanent need for help and company. In the panic state converge predisposing social and environmental factors together with intrapsychic constellations that generate a state of functional ego and representational blockage precipitating the crisis. This consists of a sudden reaction that takes the subjects by surprise: a true attack, a very intense discharge of sensations of cardiac and respiratory discomfort, and fundamentally of fear, which most of the times force them to go to a hospital or the doctor's office or to ask for urgent help to alleviate their state, which they experience as desperate.

We examine its triggering mechanisms, as well as the psychological structure of those who suffer from it. I propose that there are two times in this clinical picture: at first, a psychological one, specific to each subject, which then triggers a second time of somatic type, consisting of a massive vegetative discharge, which is specific to the species.

Whether because the coding system with which the first crisis is evoked remains activated, or because feelings of helplessness in front of significant persons are reiterated, or because the external reality exceeds the subject's capacity to face it, the result will be the experience of a fragile, weak or fragmented Ego, unable to deal with the affects and situations it must face. This

Ego plunges the subjects into a traumatic, catastrophic situation that blocks them, making it impossible for them to think, to symbolize, and therefore to solve situations. It is an overwhelming state of anguish that triggers the crisis. The persons suffering from panic try repeatedly and unsuccessfully to separate themselves, to discriminate themselves within a fusional link with a primary object with which they have an indiscriminated symbiotic relationship. The structural characteristic of such symbiotic bonds is here reviewed, highlighting that panic appears either because of the magnitude of the danger or because the libidinal bond with that object fails. As hostility towards these primary objects or their surrogates – from which the individual has not been able to differentiate and discriminate – is exacerbated, the hostile impulses turn masochistically against the subject in the form of a panic attack. Hatred and aggression are very frequent determinants and generators of conflict in these patients. They have severe difficulties in expressing these feelings verbally.

In order to understand the paralysis they experience, instead of the attack or flight reaction in the face of danger, we investigate the characteristics of the bond in comparison with the phenomena observed during hypnosis, a situation where the subject is detained in an unconscious bond of subjection to a powerful object, before which their will and psychic life are paralyzed, and their capacity to act and decide per se is taken away.

In biology, we find equivalent situations in the tonic immobility or the freezing behaviour observable before the attack of a predator. If we delve into the unconscious dynamics underlying the panic crisis, in particular its effects on the Ego, and review the conditions that precipitate it, we arrive at the concept of trauma. For psychoanalysis, trauma is a psychological response to disruptive situations which include quantitative elements (magnitude), the previous state (Ego integrity), disorganizing responses, loss of continuity (a before and an after), defencelessness, and helplessness, as well as various possibilities of recovery or elaboration.

When the Ego's response is blocked, it may lose its cohesion and become fragmented. The experienced situation of helplessness should be differentiated from that of danger. The latter is a remembered and expected situation of helplessness; anguish is then the original reaction to it, later reproduced as a sign of distress when risks are involved. Since the Ego is blocked, its capacity to emit this signal also expires, throwing it into automatic anguish, with little psychic elaboration and very primitive regression mechanisms that express in the body. This is what we observe during crises.

Traumas are also one of the effects of the pandemic. A situation that is traumatic for the Ego recognizes internal or external factors: the components of internal origin predominate in the panic crisis while the external threats (virus, contagion) prevail in the pandemic. The high frequency of panic crises during the pandemic can be explained by the joint effect of the external threat and the terror in the face of it, which reactivates intrapsychic

conflicts and states of Ego weakness enhanced both by the fear of the dis-
ease and by the consequences of the restrictive measures imposed (isolation,
social distance, generalized phobias towards any person, etc.).

There are also other common factors between the panic attack and the
pandemic. The strength and cohesion of the Ego are based on the feeling
of self, on identity. This is supported by temporal and spatial continuities
that allow the subjects to sustain themselves thanks to the recognition and
appreciation of their family, their work environment and the groups with
which they interact. Their sense of belonging, their differentiation, inclusion, and eventual participation in these spheres are also valid supports.
Extreme individualism and expanded globalization have produced a mutation in the actions and aspirations of our societies, typical of postmodernism. Indifference of the masses, neglect of private autonomy, and a certain
lack of hope for the future prevail. For their part, the isolation measures
adopted during the pandemic brought with them effects on bodies, minds,
and social bonds, with a strong impact as a result of the breakdown of
everyday life, disorganization, and the need to readjust to new conditions.

Our daily life is full of rituals, habits, and customs that play an organizing
role in our psyche. They are part of mute and invisible support of our being.
We recognize ourselves, are seen and recognized by others thanks to a conjunction of elements that give us a sign of identity. Our body, the social and
affective bonds we establish (family, partner, friendships, work), the places
we inhabit, and the values and ideals we share (language, music, clothing,
typical foods), even if they undergo changes and upheavals throughout our
lives, entail the experience of being-in-the-world and have as a correlate
to sustain us, strengthen us and provide us with a certain coherence and
self-esteem.

The restrictions imposed by the quarantine brought up a new normality.
This foundation was shaken and forced a mourning and readaptation, with
disruptive effects that caused psychic suffering in millions of people. The
pandemic threatened the survival not only of the subject but also of the species, and if we only think of the individual traumas but also of the general
responses, we are led to inquire into the psychology of the masses.

We also examine the ideals and their vicissitudes as a cause of the panic
phenomenon. Externally, in the social sphere, the subject is disconnected
from a representation established as ideal. The absence of idols and the
taboos of our time create a discontinuity in the historical fabric. Since the
Ego Ideal is a project envisioning the future, it resembles a substitute for
the ideal Ego. Once it is established, the subjective position is regulated by
a symbolic reference, which gives the Ego transcendence and is based on
its unitary character. In investigating the signifying structure in which subjects make a place for themselves, we must take into account the Ego Ideal,
according to which the subject's own identity is constituted as a function
of the recognizing look of the other. When the support of the ideal ceases

to exist, symptoms derived from the expiration of that witnessing look that sustained a project are manifested. The Ego goes through a stage of decomposition of its structure. When the bond supported by the ideal is broken, everything is possible, and it is reflected in fear of going mad, of losing control (as happens in panic). To this, the effects already mentioned, derived from the aspirations and models in force in the current culture, are added. That is why the pandemic has increased the incidence of panic.

In dealing with fanaticism, we also focus on the analysis of the mechanisms through which the Ideal operates on the minds of the subjects. The problems related to the Ideal play a key role in the genesis of fanaticism. Fanatics are fixed to an Ideal Ego conceived as a narcissistic ideal of omnipotence. This entails a primary identification with the mother invested with omnipotence. Some authors call it the "disproportion" of the ideal, intensely fixated and so obstinate that any attempt to reduce it becomes impossible. To be produced, the idealization process requires a subjective object, product of the reciprocal idealization of mother and child. It never occurs in the fanatic persons since symbolization and creation are covered in their case with the "full emptiness of certainty", where there is no separation or distance. The fanatics illusorily recover their self-esteem by adhering to an emblem or representation in an unconditional way. This representation replaces their emptiness of being or covers it under a grandiose cloak.

In the following chapter, we deal with the eroticization of danger and adventure and with adrenaline addiction. This clinical picture belongs to the group of addictions to things or behaviours and shares on this respect the description of screen addicts in the chapter on new technologies.

Addictions arise from impulses that periodically or regularly impose themselves on subjects, cannot be postponed, and lead them to seek something or carry out actions in the external world that provoke, through their psychic or biological consequences, an alteration of their affective or mental states, as is the case with drug addicts.

We assume that their psychic apparatus is unable to process any increases in tension and the anti-stimulus protection barrier is thus altered. There is an urgency to get rid of an unbearable pain, which words cannot express or calm and needs to be evacuated through action, but at the cost of affective suppression and the ever-present possibility of annihilation of the subject. These people cannot think about their conflictive situations and give them psychic figurability. This concept is analyzed in greater depth in relation to the psychic conditions that make possible the work of representation.

In these cases, adrenaline – responsible for preparing the organism, physiologically and psychically, for a situation of danger or risk – stimulates the production of dopamine in the central nervous system. This substance causes pleasure and happiness so that the individual wants to return to the activity that caused it. In dopamine "shots", we also see an analogy with what screen addicts get through their "clicks" and "likes". The production of endorphins is also stimulated by physical exercise, cycling, and swimming. To the biological effect, the psychic component of the pleasure obtained in the discharge and release of tensions through the muscular system must be added. Concomitant with the relief, the sensation of triumph and self-aggrandizement for overcoming the risk also contributes its share of pleasure and well-being. By these means of access, the search for risky situations and their overcoming become necessary to suppress experiences of pain, anguish, or emptiness.

All this is associated to the expansion of the offer and social consumption of certain sports activities, risk sports, and increasingly dangerous expeditions or adventures in natural environments as a temporary and limited way of experience.

The concept of the erogenous, its sources, and the conditions of the stimulus itself are reviewed. We see how the unpleasant, in this case, danger or risk, can become an erogenous source. In analogy with pain as an archetype or model, we articulate this with humoral processes (release of endogenous stimulating substances during physical exercise and adventure).

In the face of challenge, defiance, and confrontation, individuals test their current capacities. When struggling with the natural elements or overcoming risky situations, they experience a strong feeling of self-affirmation and power, together with relief at the disappearance of danger. They place themselves in a manic position, full of omnipotence, which apparently reverses helplessness, suffering, and neurotic unhappiness.

The search for new and vivifying sensations, together with experiences of purity, counteracts the states of anguish, oppression, and confinement. Autoerotic and sensory stimulation not only averts these states but also reorders the narcissistic balance on a bodily and sensory basis, and thus sustains the feeling of self-integrity – particularly when this is compromised by life circumstances – and in this way constitutes an energetic purification valve conducive to feelings of well-being.

We dive into the organization and structure of the fanatic mind, as well as into the factors that generate and boost fanaticism in the inter- and trans-subjective worlds. In this chapter, we draw on other disciplinary sources, such as sociology and literature. To understand the present incidence and expansion of fanaticism – which, like panic, is of long standing – social and cultural aspects (globalization, tendency towards uniformity, clash of civilizations, breakdown and changes in values, ideals, and paradigms) are very important, as well as the presence of some varieties different from the classic religious ones, such as political or sports fanaticism (analyzed here in a more exhaustive way).

The sociological concept of fundamentalism is made explicit as a reaction against the changes of modernity, experienced as a threat that seeks to dissolve archaic and traditional identities and values (the observance and certainties of which would bring peace and security) whose return and validity are deeply desired.

Four elements compose and agitate the fanatic mind: passions, beliefs, problems of being, and, finally, group dynamics and the need for identification.

The passionate experience (different from the amorous one) drags the subjects to a state where their reason is swept away, and criticism disappears. It is as if they were enchanted, surrendered to a unique irreplaceable object for which they have an imperious need. They wish an oceanic fusion with it; limits disappear in a joyful union that captures them almost completely. They need it as an identifying support, but they must immolate their thought as the price for this surrender that will give them total certainty, absence of doubt, and infinite security. The bond is totally asymmetrical and alienating, but it illusorily distances them from any suffering and conflict.

Beliefs occupy a central place in fanatical thinking. They are established in the psychic organization by family and social influences. They also fulfil an integrating function since sharing a set of beliefs provides bonds of identity and a sense of belonging.

Religious beliefs allow us to see how the Ego can satisfy its desires through thought without falling into delirium or creating a work of art. The subjects adhere to them when their unconscious fantasies, endowed with a strong desiderative quantum, make the Ego grant them a reality. This is how beliefs acquire power over mental functioning. All beliefs are based on probability and not on certainty, but they have as their correlate an emotional state of security that accompanies the certainty.

Fanatics have no doubts but an obstinate and almost delirious certainty. They adhere to an overvalued idea or emblem that leads them to cancel their own thinking and that of others. Their ideas are imbued with omnipotence; their objects, idealized beyond discussion, endowed with the most precious qualities, are born of heartbreaking experiences of emptiness. This mortar welds the fanatics to their ideas. The fanatic ideas (characterized by some authors as "maximum ideas") are also "monoideas", with scarce associations and associative trade; isolation, together with obstinacy, are its characteristics; they are dogmatically fierce and rigid ideas. They act as a painkiller in the face of suffering. They simplify facts and situations seeking to impose themselves on the authoritarian model, unlike authoritative ideas that are valued because they come from someone respected.

As to the need for identification, religious or political fanatics are permanently dependent on an external figure since they feel worthless. They may give their life or kill for that external figure on whom they depend and whom they consider all-powerful and infallible.

The emblem gives the fanatics anchorage and support, and they fuse with it; however, they perceive their inner emptiness and their poor self-esteem. They feel threats to the emblem as threats to their own Ego, which leads them to take refuge in sheltering groups or institutions to which they give their heart and life.

It is important to understand the passage from the individual to the social: by joining institutions, groups, or sects, loneliness is dissipated along with doubts and weaknesses; the individual obtains security and thus becomes even more fanatical.

The pathology of narcissism allows us to understand that with this fusion, the subject manages to expand the limits of the Ego, which now comes to encompass the mass of followers. In such a context, hatred functions as a cement that binds, fixes, and solidifies. As paranoid feelings intensify, violence becomes inevitable since emptiness and dehumanization are projected onto the opponent, and evil, insensitivity towards the other and criminal behaviour make their appearance.

Fanaticism develops slowly in the intimacy of the home and then embraces all spheres of the personality. Fanatics have serious deficits in the constitution of the self, with a hyper-present mother, unable to tolerate absences – similar to what happens with screen addicts. There are no cuts or exclusions, but their capacity to think, to symbolize, is annulled, governed by the bond that imprisons and sustains them at the same time. Intolerable feelings are expelled out. There is always a figure full of qualities and power that is a model of identification – passive for masochists, active for those who will become leaders. This intrusive model leads them to effectively repeat orders and commands. They lack subjective freedom and do not experience mourning processes.

Our chapter provides clinical examples of sports fanaticism: adhesion in different formats (supporter, adherent, and fanatic), ritualized participation every weekend, and the club T-shirt as a badge of identity that is transmitted from parents to children.

In the chapter on new technologies, the modes of psychic structuring are examined according to the models and theories of several psychoanalytical authors and some from other currents (R. Spitz and K. Lorenz), comparing the differences introduced by the visual world.

The subjective constitution is established in exchange with others. We speculate on what varies, is altered, or prevails when that predominant other is a machine and not a human since, in order to constitute itself, the human psyche must be open to stimuli coming from the outside. We take advantage of the contributions of authors who subscribe the theory of communication and linguistics (Habermas, Jakobson, and Austin) as well as those by Humberto Eco and Alain Touraine. The effects of the verbal and the visual are compared, as well as the brain areas stimulated by each of them, and it is shown how the subject's perception and posture vary in each case. It is highlighted how through the mass media, captured by images, the subjects tend to become passive, decathect the body, and are reduced to being voyeurs. The machines offer a homogeneous model, which does not vary according to the cultural characteristics of each social group and which the public supports and accepts uncritically. Symbols and functional myths reduce individuality to a minimum and the emotional, instead of being symbolized, represented, is induced, manipulated. This resembles the hypnoid and addictive effect of religious ideologies, which also provide the illusion of participation and belonging.

This is one of the nuclei that fanatical personalities and sects adopt to oppose this "destruction of idiosyncrasy" by violent groups seeking identity, purity, or simply the vindication of certain values and cultures.

Based on linguistics, we highlight the performative aspect of language, particularly digital language. It provokes and enhances subjective facts and subtracts itself from the mere representative reality. It brings the subject into existence. The Web creates a very wide avenue for these modes of subjective presence, making it easier for subjects to find themselves, to be seen, named, and located by others – and this is one of the reasons for its enormous addictive power.

We also discuss digital communication and its effects and the difference between speech acts and those of visual communication. The latter exist in an ahistorical space with no territory, with signs that lose their referential charge and lead to changes in the structures of representation and bonding.

We point out the incompatibility of the word with the image. In a culture that values the reified, global image, being seen as a synonymous with being, the subjectivity, symbolically inconsistent, is compensated through the body image, linked to the manifestation of sensations as an expressive mode: it may be plainly observed in those who seek vivifying sensations through sport, adventure, and risk. The analysis of pornography allows us to understand the impact of erotically charged images on the subjects, who are fascinated, and avid; they need to repeat incessantly the effect of monosemic, ahistorical current images that allow them to have the illusion of participation and to be narcissistically identified, but also exposed to see everything without cuts or concealment, in a traumatic way. The subjects make clear their longing to look at an object in order to feel close to it. It is an object that is not there but which they feel they control and dominate at will. Unlike a human being, who may be and not be there, the machine is always present.

We also focus on the effects caused by virtual reality and its differences with material reality, as well as the impact this has on subjectivity. Through virtual reality, experiences of anguish, discomfort, and fragmentation are replaced by others of presence and power. The way this is done is equivalent to that of adrenaline addicts since the narcissistic pleasure, the feeling of power, and the effect on endogenous stimulant amines all lead to an equivalent sensation.

There is a flight from everyday reality, a narcissistic withdrawal, a submersion in a partly playful space, where the passage of time, dependence on another human being and helplessness are also denied. All of which counteracts loneliness and helplessness. Its effect is similar to that of the coral fishes described by K. Lorenz, who perceive themselves by looking at others like themselves. They perceive and constitute themselves simultaneously.

We propose that the set of the above mechanisms (stimuli, compulsion, adrenaline shots, hyperpresence, withdrawal symptoms, to be induced into an addictive bond) is equivalent to the relationship with a hyperpresent mother that overrides or flattens thinking and incite the subject to be passively fascinated and pending on the machine. There is no space left to form internal representations since the absence/presence register is altered, and the reality principle (or the true/false difference) ceases to act.

It is also significant that social networking companies exploit this psychological weakness to add users. The addictive circuit is organized when intense sources of pleasure mobilize an insatiable greed, where the thing seen is confused with the thing itself (as happens with pornographic images), leading to the endless and incessant repetition of such images since the inherent basic frustration never disappears.

Finally, the quality of such bonds is, as in the case of the fanatic, asymmetrical, since the subject has a compelling need to merge with an object that soothes his inner emptiness, his intolerable sense of non-being. The latter is not only an object of desire: it is needed to conjure everything – anguish, discomfort – and also to provide the individual with self-esteem, which he lacks. The question is to be, to be taken into account, to generate something in the other, in anyone.

The objects on the screens do not respect the uniqueness.

In the chapter on the pandemic, we examine its psychic effects, stressing that it has been a unique experience in the history of mankind, both in terms of the number of people affected and the threat and risk it has posed to the human race.

As we have done with panic, we examine the conditions of trauma (magnitude, previous state, disorganizing response, discontinuity, defencelessness, and helplessness). We review the factors that transform the everyday and normal modes of reaction of individuals, leading them to function regressively in archaic and primitive modes when being part of a mass. This mass functioning is caused by a situation of crisis or threat (pandemic), one of whose components, fear, is enhanced by the mass media and by the global use of technology, as well as by the intervention of the State as guarantor and controller of people's lives and actions. This produces, both in the individuals and the masses, phenomena such as passivity and blind obedience to authority. Aspects such as cohesion, the libidinal bond together with hypnotic seduction (already discussed in dealing with panic), the relationship with the ideal (an aspect we saw regarding fanaticism), thinking in images (examined in relation to new technologies), and a credulous acceptance of slogans. This set of elements is very similar to those we explored when discussing the virtual world.

The media have an enormous impact on certain psychic strata, whether with their real news or with fake news. Fear is a trigger, as are images that support sexual arousal and allow its manipulation. We study the power relationship between subjects and the State and its history, the varieties of power bonds, and their modalities (training, domination, reward, punishment), widely observed during the present pandemic. We review Milgram's experiment, according to which the essence of obedience lies in the fact that persons consider themselves to be the instrument of the realization of the desires of others and detach themselves from their individual responsibility.

We recall that Freud, in his work on the Army and the Church as models of artificial masses, argued that both share the illusion of having a boss, a paternal substitute who cares for all and keeps the mass united. This libidinal model preserves from the experience of anguish and panic due to the breakdown of affective bonds. We also underline these concepts in the chapter on fanaticism with respect to adhesion to the emblem and indicate that its effects are self-preservation as well as protection against disintegration, emptiness, and anguish.

The pandemic affected bodies, minds, and social bonds due to the rupture of everyday life and the need to readjust to a new reality. Rituals, habits, and daily customs serve to sustain identity; they are mute and invisible support of our being and fulfil a stabilizing function for our psyche.

In this sense, the time factor is one of the most important vectors. Rituals have to do with becoming aware of the passage of time; restriction measures and diluted temporal limits generate states of disorientation. In psychoanalysis, the notion of time is worked on having into account the modifications in its perception brought about by the pandemic (a continuous present, an indefinite time, a timeless state, a dead infinite time, urgency) that is associated with states of uneasiness, helplessness, and defencelessness already discussed in other chapters. We emphasize that in the pandemic, there was a temporality different from the chronological one, the experiential time. Likewise, we delve conceptually into Prygogine's chaos theory and its application to the concepts of psychoanalytic theory.

We understand the vicissitudes of individuals, families, and societies as complex structures, which go through processes of disorganization, destabilization, chaos, and spontaneous restructuring, and these are appreciable in very diverse areas (such as communication, bonds, work, and organizations consistent with a new normality). People had to assimilate restrictions, to live mourning, and to open up to new tools in order to learn the new, and by transforming it, to transform themselves. We delve into the concept of uncertainty, which also evokes the experience of helplessness. Humanity learned to defend itself from uncertainty with the edifice of culture; but in the current situation, the absence of conclusive answers coming from the power and knowledge of science has injured our narcissism and our cultural ideals, increasing anxiety, fear, and the feeling of perplexity. This was expressed in fear of contagion, of being hospitalized, deprived, and restricted from carrying out the actions and exchanges common in subjectivizing contexts. The perplexity is manifested as a conscious manifestation of the principle of uncertainty and the suffering linked to unpredictability.

A crucial fact is the possibility of continuing to recognize oneself as belonging to a given space and time within an organization of relationships. We ask ourselves: how can we protect ourselves from uncertainty? To find an answer, we turn to Spinoza's philosophy and his vision of hope, linked to the tolerance of uncertainty and to being able to mourn for what has been lost. Thus a path of exploration of new modalities can begin. The reassuring memories of how the crisis was faced converge with the affective bonds giving rise to a support mesh or network.

Chapter 1

Panic attack

Although the symptoms of this condition are known since ancient times, its incidence has grown very significantly in recent years, to the point that it is considered that a third of the world's population suffers or will suffer at some point from this disorder.

Its name is derived from the Greek *Panikós* and from Pan, the god of fields, forests, and shepherds, a faun with feet and horns of goats, to whose activity the unknown noises of nature were attributed (it was said that Pan used a very noisy stratagem to repel his enemies, who ended up fleeing in terror). Since then, unfounded or excessive terror has been called *panic*. Pan's task was to lead by night the round of nymphs, whom he pursued with amorous advances, making him both desirable and feared. Christianity takes up the figure of Pan associated with the sinister, the satanic. It is represented by the goat of the covens. On the other hand, the Greek prefix "pan-" means the totality (as in *Pan-American*) and also the personality as a whole, which is disarticulated and devastated during crises.

The significant increase in consultations on account of panic attacks has led to a more detailed analysis of its symptomatology as well as the conditions of its genesis. Several authors have proposed that certain social and environmental factors contribute to its emergence; in my view, these are combined with intrapsychic dispositions and constellations that converge in a state of functional Ego and representational blockage that precipitates the crisis. Because of its high frequency, we can include it within the "fashionable" clinical pictures, those that call the attention of physicians and psychologists, making them suspect that in these thunderous "cries for help" hysterical phantoms could be underlying. The clinical pictures presented by many patients do not correspond to the real panic attack; they are usually intense somatic manifestations of anguish or distress, while others are expressions of "contagion" or identification.

Panic is a sudden, untimely reaction. It is affect-specific, constitutes a global reaction of the Ego, and reveals a very intense somatic engagement. The subjects actually suffer an attack that takes them by surprise, like a bombardment of very intense sensations of predominantly cardiac

DOI: 10.4324/9781003293569-2

discomfort (palpitations, heart shaking, or increased heartbeats), but there can also be thoracic oppression or pain, suffocation or lack of breath.

The first descriptions of the panic attack were made in soldiers in 1871 by a military physician, Jacob Mendes Da Costa, who had witnessed it during the American Civil War. (It was then called "Da Costa's syndrome" or "syndrome of irritable heart".) This physician observed that, during or after combat, individuals presented a series of mainly cardiac symptoms (precordial oppression, palpitations, and choking sensation) of a non-organic nature; he later labelled it as an "anxiety disorder" and stated that the bodily symptoms were a reaction of the autonomic nervous system to something that the subject perceived as dangerous. Fear was another of its *princeps* expressions: fear to die, to go crazy, to lose the sense, to lose the control of oneself, to faint after having feelings of instability and dizziness. Other individuals manifest tremors, tingling, chills or suffocation, nausea, choking sensation, and profuse sweating. These symptoms have their peak in the first ten minutes, are usually accompanied by a feeling of de-realization or depersonalization, and then progressively diminish.

But the tremendous shock and imbalance they cause force the individuals to stop any activity they are doing. If they are driving a car, they must stop it completely and not resume driving it right away; if they are going somewhere, they must cancel their plans; if they are traveling by bus or train, they must abandon the means of transport and seek shelter where they may receive professional attention. In these circumstances, the subjects feel mentally and physically affected, overwhelmed by a state that paralyzes them and after which they are totally defenceless. They cannot make any decision. Therefore, they need to urgently ask for help to mitigate their state.

Triggering situations, structure, Ego

Analytical work with numerous patients who presented this picture allowed me to infer that there was a common set of situations that triggered these crises. These situations were clearly of a psychological nature and absolutely unique for each patient. It can be safely said that there are two phases in panic attacks; the first one is psychological and acts as a trigger for a second phase, predominantly somatic, which is what accounts for all the symptoms described above. There is a biological response here, typical of the species, more or less common to all individuals once the psycho-neuro-humoral mechanism that activates it has been triggered. It consists of a massive vegetative discharge. Several authors agree in this, such as De Masi (2004), who literally states that the panic crisis has, above all, a psychic origin but triggers a specific and automatic neurobiological response (mind/body relationship). He points out two moments in the crisis: one in which the anguish is noticed at the psychical level and a second one in which bodily participation prevails and terror transforms it into automatic and uncontrollable distress. For this author, the panic attack is not necessarily the result of the mobilization of emotional conflicts, but is based on primitive, automatic, and preverbal mechanisms, which are therefore, on many occasions, independent of any conflict.

Likewise, H. Bleichmar (2016) says that conflicts and traumas are not enough to trigger panic attacks. He speaks of necessary and sufficient conditions for this to happen. The conflict and the traumatic situation operating in the unconscious are sufficient conditions, but to this must be added the specificity of the neurovegetative reaction and, above all, "the encoding made about what dangers the anguish would entail". Once the first panic attack takes place, the distress does not depend only on the causes that originated it but "on the evocation of the traumatic situation under which the attack was registered".

In *Inhibition, Symptom and Anxiety* (1926), Freud differentiated between automatic and signal anxiety (or anguish). The panic attack can be understood as corresponding to a psychobiological imbalance (in this sense, it would be equivalent to the automatic anguish); then, when the bodily manifestations or the conflicts or unconscious situations that were present at its inception are activated again in the unconscious and the consciousness, they anticipate to the subject that the panic attack may repeat itself. Therefore, it would be what Strachey, in translating Freud, called a "signal anxiety": the anguish arises before an indicator or signal connected with the situation originally causing the panic attack. Therefore, when the individuals unconsciously assume that there is or will be an interpersonal conflict, or perceive their own anger and hostility towards the other – making them anticipate an aggressive response, such as punishment or abandonment –, or feel sexual excitement for the fears that this response may cause, or fantasize about narcissistically abandoning an object they simultaneously feel as protective, or consider themselves incapable of facing some task or assuming a certain responsibility, all this is for them a sign that a panic attack may occur, because these conditions preceded the first crisis and the subsequent ones. Not only that conflictive situation produces anguish but the subjects codify it as a possible trigger of the attack.

The basic representation is that the self is in danger, not only because of the anguish but because of the various causes that originate it and keep it active. The subjects can arrive at this representation by fixation to the traumatic situation in which they felt powerless in front of meaningful figures or a threatening external reality or before parental discourses that, by identification, place them in that imaginary place.

Lenarduzzi (2005), in turn, poses the presence of "intense feelings of helplessness that translate into an automatic and devastating anguish as a result of external or internal excitations that the self is unable to control". The anguish signal is an achievement of self-preservation; it makes the individual to be on the alert to danger so that the Ego may set in motion its defences and does not become disorganized. Both kind of anguishes, the automatic and the signal, emphasize psychic helplessness. And the panic emphasizes that condition. For this author, the psychological theories alone are not enough to account for all the humoral and behavioural manifestations; to explain their genesis, she believes it is necessary to include the complementary series and the psychosomatic vulnerability. The crisis would add a new motive for anguish since the Ego feels abandoned by its body, which does not respond to it and seems to escape the control of the mind.

This results in increased self-observation, with secondary hypochondria due to an accumulation of narcissistic libido. The capacity to symbolize as well as to give meaning to what is happening is temporarily suspended. The whole thing causes the sensation of being immersed in madness. Lenarduzzi quotes Winnicott when he says that "one does not fear a future madness but one that has already been experienced. One fears its return". That original madness had been experienced, due to an environmental fault, in a very early stage of psychic development, when it was not possible to understand what was happening. The panic attack would reedit that catastrophic circumstance.

However, according to Bolognini, it must be taken into account that the dynamics of the acute anxiety attack does not have an absolute psychogenetic specificity and does not seem to be reducible to a single explanatory formula. In the literature, there is no key to solve the enigma of this pathology, which is likely to have multiple causes, comparable as a symptom to fever or fainting.

One of the keys to understand panic is that which occurs with the Ego of the suffering subject. In all cases, it is taken by surprise, overwhelmed, and devastated. Add to this that the subject is often in a traumatic situation, and many of the metapsychological explanations that have been developed focus on the effects and psychic consequences of such phenomena. The characteristics and preconditions of this Ego also explain another of the peculiar signs of a panic attack: the phenomenon of mental and motor paralysis.

Heinz Kohut (1971) studied patients who suffered from specific self-disturbances and developed, as a result, narcissistic pathologies. These subjects presented very early disruptions in the relationship with their (idealized) objects, which generated a general structural weakness (deficient or malfunctioning anti-stimulus barrier). This weakness interferes with the psyche's ability to maintain the basic narcissistic homeostasis of the personality and results in oscillations in the cohesion of the self. Subjects may remain fixed to archaic configurations of a grandiose self or in overrated, narcissistically cathected archaic objects, which nevertheless are not integrated with the rest of the personality. Archaic objects invested with narcissistic libido (called by Kohut "objects of the self") are not considered as distinct beings, independent of the self. In these patients' regressive stages, it is possible to observe disturbances in their corporeal sensation and in their perception of themselves; there is also degeneration of their language, concretization, and fracture of their thought processes. All this is called "narcissistic vulnerability".

Diamond (1985) believes that the common element of panic attacks, hypochondria, and agoraphobia is the threat to the consistency and cohesion of the self, expressed by the patients as the fear of not being themselves anymore or of falling apart. The true underlying core would be their fragility and potential self-fragmentation.

Busch et al. (1995) highlight the weakness of the self and its defences beyond the Oedipal period. Individuals exposed to panic experience feel that they are unable to modulate or manage internal tensions and external stimuli when terrified and consider themselves inept to carry out normal evolutionary tasks, especially those related to separation and autonomy. The background psychodynamic framework of the panic crisis would follow the following sequence: (1) Threat of collapse of a false self. (2) Risk of visible or invisible symbiosis, either in the present or in the near future. (3) The subjective experience is that of approaching a conflictive and feared traumatic area, as in phobias. In all these cases, the alarm about the breakdown of the defensive system will be all the more dramatic, the more unconscious, tenacious, and primitive in form and time has been its genesis.

It may be added that even if there were mechanisms that regulated a precarious tolerance to anguish since childhood (giving rise to the vulnerability of the self to its fragmentation), the subject may have established an acceptably cohesive self thanks to compensatory defensive structures. But if these structures are weakened, cohesion is lost, and the experience of internal fragmentation gives rise to panic. Likewise, as a consequence of long-term states of panic, there is a regression to pre-cohesion stages, in which there is an urgent need for objects of the self adequate for that development period, so early disturbed.

Let's present a clinical vignette. Alberto, 35 years old, a businessman, married, and with two children aged 12 and 5, lives happily with his family, is prosperous at his work, but every now and then has episodes of panic attack like the ones described. He dreaded these crises, which were absolutely inexplicable to him. He demanded a psychopharmacological prescription to confront them because "if not, I'll go crazy".. since he was looking for the "magic medicine", a drug that emded his crisis, it was vey difficult to install him in the analytic process putting words, feelings and associations that linked the crisis with (situations or vicissitudes) of his present and in a second stage to epiosdes of his childhood history. Through free association, the situations that triggered the crisis began to appear: strong arguments with his parents, a hypertensive crisis of his father with a danger of death, etc. Alberto was paralyzed by the hatred he felt against his father, with whom he maintained a childish bond of hostility and submission. The same happened with his mother, always busy with her own needs and absorbed in her hypochondriac worries, who neglected him since he was a very young child. In addition, she would verbally assault him every time Alberto disagreed with her (trying to discriminate himself).

Terror and panic confront people like Alberto with the uncanny character of their archaic ties (Bolognini, 2010). The conflict they endure takes place in the realm of Ego integrity. It is there that Green rescues (The Work of the Negative) (1999) the Freudian idea that "the genuine models of the relationship of hate come from the struggle of the self to preserve and assert itself". It may be said that in the panic, there are failed and repetitive attempts to resolve this conflict, which has to do predominantly with self-preservation. Structurally, and following the Kohutian model, they are patients whose narcissistic organization is weak and who tend to establish fusional and idealized links with libidinal objects, with a strong subject/object indiscrimination. When some intense conflictive situation is activated with the primary objects or their surrogates in daily life (bosses, etc.) – particularly when the hostility towards these objects is exacerbated, from which they have not been able to separate/discriminate themselves completely, being lived as parts of their own self – , the hostile impulses, which cannot be derived towards the outside, turn masochistically against the subject himself in the form of a panic attack (as its name says, it is a true "attack".) To truly separate themselves from these objects would lead these subjects to run the risk of a catastrophic Ego disintegration, since they feel they have no resources to face another way of being in the world and of connecting with it. Acted or verbalized hatred, attack, and even flight become impossible. Hence, they suffer from that self-disintegration which is the panic attack, along with all its consequences – that is to say, it is the body who reacts, as the Ego is unable to express the distress or conflict on a more psychic or bonding level, with actions in the external world. The traumatic event represented by the panic attack is felt by the subject as a sure cause of death, the last signal emitted by the Ego before being overwhelmed. In other words, although the event does not cause death, the sensation of death signals the immediate and transitory eclipse of the Ego. For the Ego, death is only representable as absence itself.

Internal bonding structure, symbiosis

Mahler (2000) focused his studies on the processes of separation-individuation, describing in young children a symbiotic organization with little representational differentiation of self and object. The experience of separation would entail a primitive panic whose specific defence would be the establishment of the symbiotic organization, situation in which the child tries to make the mother behave as an extension of his/her own body. Early disruptions of the symbiosis imply the risk of suffering panic experiences, with the anguish of disintegration, loss of the sense of being an entity and of identity, fear of being swallowed up and annulled by the symbiotic object turned into a persecutory one by projection, beyond the labile limits of the self and of the non-neutralized destructive aggressiveness.

Other authors have described symbiotic nuclei or structures in patients suffering from panic attacks. They refer to both the quality of interpersonal and intersubjective bonds and the manifestations that appear in transference during treatment (Ferro, 1996; Bolognini, 2010). They emphasize that the withdrawal of interpersonal investments and the loss of the integral sense of a functional unit are observed. Although the quantitative aspect of the bonds (libidinal quota at stake) is important, the most relevant thing is, specifically, the quality and structure of the internal relations of the subject.

In *Mass Psychology and Analysis of the Ego* (1921), when speaking of the cohesive functioning of an army in relation to panic, Freud refers to allegorical group representations, useful to explore the inner functional *group mind*. He points out that "Panic arises if this mass [the army] falls apart. Orders of the superiors are ignored and each one is concerned only with himself without paying attention to the others". Freud concentrates on cases where the group is panicked even when danger does not exceed established or usually tolerated limits. "If we take the word panic in the sense of collective fear, we can establish a broad analogy. Distressing fear is provoked in the individual either by the magnitude of the danger or by the suppression of emotional ties (libidinal cathexes). The latter is the case of neurotic anguish". The analogy is suggestive if we think that, in the individual who is about to suffer a panic attack, the functional bonds between the parts of the self are already ineffective, with little cohesion among them (the same as in an army or in a sports team nowadays).

Baumgart's (2010) reflection on the functioning of the ideal in these cases is interesting. When a sum of individuals places a single and same object as their Ego ideal, they identify themselves with each other and a social bond is born. "Panic reveals a short circuit in the idealization and sublimation process, through disconnection from the ideal". The intense fear takes on gigantic proportions, unrelated to the magnitude of the danger. The essence of panic consists of having no relation to the threatening danger. The relaxation of the libidinous structure of the mass means that the ideal has fallen down, and any relationship with one's fellow creatures is left out of balance. The Ego echoes that danger.

These Freudian concepts anticipated those of cohesion (Kohut) and of the inner group mind. Within the subject, there is a pluri-objective relational network.

Aggressiveness, hatred, subject-object discrimination

I have observed that aggressiveness is a very frequent and crucial problem in these patients. They have serious difficulty in exteriorizing it, particularly with those objects with which they have established a strong libidinal bond.

The inquiry into this aspect in the course of the sessions made it possible to detect real-life situations that increased the feeling of hatred and, sometimes, the desire for death towards people in the immediate environment (parents, children, or their surrogates.) These feelings were consciously experienced as catastrophic and unacceptable. Moreover, it was impossible to verbalize them directly in those bonds, which mobilized in the subjects an intense anguish that later on led to panic.

As we saw in Alberto's case, the experience of hatred has a double face in these cases. On the one hand, it is at the service of discrimination, autonomy, and self-preservation; but, on the other hand, as it takes place without a suitable Ego base or support to tolerate the separation from these symbiotic/functional/idealized objects, it only launches them into a mission that is impossible at the time. The experiences of disintegration and annihilation prevail; it is as if the individual were ejected into a terrifying void where there is no time, no form, no content, or continent.

In the course of his third year of analysis, Alberto referred to the sinister margins among which he had to move in order "not to kill or be killed" when he told his mother that "they would celebrate Mother's Day at noon in the house of their in-laws, and would go later to greet her". Scandal, offense, intolerable relegation, betrayal: these were the feelings she launched to him like darts he could neither avoid nor struggle with, but in spite of everything he decided, with the support of his wife and children, to take action. During that week's sessions, an attenuated panic crisis was the price he had to pay and suffer, by way of words, without having a *"grand mal"*. The mere fact of holding and receiving his feelings and experiences transmitted through words provided him with support, an Ego-prosthesis, in the transference.

Greenson (1959) considers that panic is a state of psychic impotence with reduction of the Ego functions and loss of cathexis of the internal and external objects until a regression to a state of lack of object may occur (perhaps by stimulation of a primitive hostility that leads to the temporary destruction or disinvestment of the internal objects).

In Bion's model (Ferro, 1996), the psychic apparatus is confronted with experiences or mental contents that are qualitatively uncontained by the structure itself and/or qualitatively indigestible through the transforming capacity of the insufficient alpha function.

In a Cornell University study, with 25 cases of children at risk of panic-related disorganization, it was observed that their neurophysiological vulnerability exposed them to an increased fear of the strange and unknown, often linked to a traumatic experience or diathesis. These children had basic feelings of inadequacy and anxious dependence on caretakers; if the parental support was also inadequate, they became angry with the parents and feared that their own aggressiveness could destroy them. This pre-Oedipal conflict is added to the subsequent Oedipal ones, aggravating the situation. Competitive aggressiveness with the parent of the same sex, fantasies of personal success, or its realization can cause attacks, with regression to states of impotence and dependence. It leads to a vicious circle since this regressive situation is experienced as dangerous because it is associated with fantasized fears of passive homosexuality, can be followed by an aggressive Oedipal reaction which makes the situation even worse, and so on. The panic would be the result of these conflicting forces, aggravated by the perception of an ill-tolerated relational regression. (According to Bolognini, this may occur only in some cases.) They also have difficulty recognizing emotions such as anger (Vangaard, 1989) that are feared to be uncontrollable and, therefore, isolated. This leads to defensive shielding and loss of the signal anxiety, exposing them to a direct passage from insensitivity to a massive and overwhelming experience. The vicious circle is the weakness of the Ego – fear of autonomy – intolerance of dependence – untouchability of affects – deactivation of the signal anxiety. The subjects try to convince themselves that they are healthy and strong. They make use of counterphobic defences. They are afraid of being afraid.

Bonding, paralysis

One of the most relevant facts in the panic attack is the effect of mental and motor paralysis in the face of danger. One could ask why the reaction is paralysis and not attack or escape, which are more active mechanisms of response. Perhaps the comparison with the state of hypnosis produced by terror will shed some light on these mechanisms.

Freud and Breuer, in *Studies on Hysteria* (1895), refer to the void of consciousness generated by hypnosis and by several psychic disturbances, such as that produced by terror. He says that terror produces self-hypnosis. In "Mass Psychology and Analysis of the Ego", Freud (1921) states that hypnosis adds a supplementary paralysis derived from the relationship between a person of greater power and a powerless and helpless one. The "hypnoid state" of the immature Ego, which is captured in an unconscious bond of submission to the object, generates a traumatic state, a "terror neurosis" where the will of the subject is taken away and his/her psychic life is paralyzed.

We can equate this bonding character of hypnosis with that of the person suffering a panic attack. The difference would be that in hypnosis, there is a clearer discrimination between subject and object. The person who suffers a panic attack is likely to have a narcissistic type of organization, with fusion and indiscrimination between subject and object, as we have said. This bonding situation is expressed both in the intersubjective and in the intrasubjective areas. To remain frozen, dazed, and paralyzed by fear is a common involuntary reaction of the body, even though fighting or running away seems to be the most adequate thing to do. This cerebral response has a name in biology: tonic immobility. In animals, it is considered an evolutionary adaptation to a predator's attack when it is not possible to resist, and there are no other resources available. It is called *freezing behavior*. The paralysis caused by fear occurs, for example, in a kind of goats that, in situations of danger, "freeze" and fall to the ground as solid blocks so that the predator ignores them. Obviously, this does not usually happen. These goats exist precisely because of their genetic characteristic to remain paralyzed so that the rest of the herd escapes. A similar behaviour is also seen in dogs when faced with a threat: they lay on the ground before the herd's leader as a sign of submission, letting it see that they do not represent a threat. But although this behaviour has been widely observed in animals, it has not yet been studied in humans. Experts describe it as a temporary state of motor immobility in response to a situation of extreme fear that often occurs in cases of rape and other traumatic events, such as abuse, mugging, assault, or serious accidents. In human panic, the paralyzing reaction is both physical and emotional and affects the whole individual, who gives in and is left defenceless.

Panic and traumatic situation

These patients also have serious difficulty in tolerating anguish. Those who develop phobias, for example, have the ability to generate the defensive mechanisms that will prevent the invasion of anguish (MBaranger, personal communication). Here this capacity is affected, and from the signal anguish, there is a short path to automatic anguish due to the overflowing of the Ego response capacity. Panic is considered by many authors as a severe crisis of anguish, but as we have been saying, it is much more than that. The explosion of uncontained automatic anguish installs the subject in a traumatic situation. By altering the dynamic equilibrium of drives, it contributes to unbind what the libido has bound, releasing a certain quantity of the death drive. Part of this free death drive, which can take the form of destructiveness, is distributed over the psyche as a whole; it detaches itself from its Superego anchorage and exerts its action in a dramatic way. The anchorages of the representative systems – both of the psychic representatives of the drive (the affects) and of the representations of objects – are also lost. When the outward discharge or flight is prevented, an inner vegetative discharge is produced. All this is often experienced as a sensation of imminent death, of annihilation. There is no possibility of thinking, of symbolizing. The greater the traumatic effect, the closer the experience of unnamed terror or pure trauma (Baranger and Mom, 1987) in its economic modelling.

What is the traumatic situation for the Ego? It is that which makes it lose its cohesion. It can be of internal or external origin. Wars, natural catastrophes, economic crises with material losses (home, work, goods, nuclear family) or bodily damages, the obligation to leave behind safe and known shelters or stable references; affective losses, mourning, separations: all these situations differ from those that predominate in individuals with a narcissistic structure of personality or structural weakness of the Ego, as we have described. Following M. and W. Baranger, "in psychoanalytic terms a trauma is always an early traumatic situation that does not only threatens the subject and reveals the existence of a break in his/her anti-stimulus barrier; it is a vital situation of helplessness, that is to say, a world of inter-human relations and of relations of object, that are not necessarily the same thing". In turn, the traumatic situation is that of a loss (of the mother or of her love, of the love of objects, of the Superego, etc.), and these experiences plunge the subject into a state of powerlessness, of total motor or mental impotence, in the face of the irruption of stimuli of external or internal origin. The basic traumatic situation is that of helplessness. This must be differentiated from the dangerous situation, in which the helplessness is discerned, remembered, and expected. The original response to helplessness is anguish, later reproduced as a cry for help in a situation of danger.

It is important to include the notion of "cumulative trauma" developed by Masud Khan and quoted by M. and W. Baranger (1987). It results from the tensions and stresses the child experiences in the context of his or her Ego dependence on the mother, who is both a protective barrier and an auxiliary self. "Gaps in its function as a barrier are silently and imperceptibly present throughout the developmental process. They are neither observable nor understood as traumas at the moments when they occur, and they do not acquire the character of traumas but by accumulation and retrospectively". These concepts, also derived from Winnicott, suggest the mother's crumbling or failing in her role of dosing and regulating internal and external stimuli; thus, a situation of invasion is reached that has a disruptive effect on the organization and integration of the Ego.

Together with Klein, Balint, and Winnicott, this author places himself in an object-oriented approach to trauma that leads him to confuse what is traumatic with what is pathogenic. Another school of thought leads to an economic model, without an object or unrelated to an object, where there is a break in the anti-stimulus barrier, flooding of estimuli of unmanageable magnitude, and a total and absolute helplessness. It generates a devastating automatic anguish; it is a pure, disruptive, senseless trauma. The repetition of the panic experience, to the extent that it cannot be remembered (even if it is a posteriori, historically) and become meaningful in some way, keeps alive the influence of the Thanatotic, of that which has been compulsively reiterated and not linked. It is always possible to find threads, associations, and triggers of one kind or another that make it possible to inscribe what happens in some significant context so as to stop the disorganizing and paralyzing invasion. There is always a first time of the trauma, the pre-traumatic, which gets its etiological value from the second, from its being reactivated by another event, perhaps trivial but dateable and nameable, and by the analytical historization linking both. The first time of the trauma remains mute until it is later (*nachtraglichkeit*) allowed to speak and constitute itself as a trauma. The mute, pre-traumatic time of the trauma is as difficult to assimilate, as unrepresentable and unnameable as the death drive itself. The pathogenic effects of the traumatic situation, the symptoms, are no more than failed attempts to link, by making it speak, the part of the death drive that has not been able nor will ever be able to become a coherent discourse.

The experience of panic in itself can be a trauma included in the mind through a more or less tiring work and then functioning as such a posteriori. It can be a phobic object that memory must avoid. Pao (1979) describes five subsequent phases: (1) an unsustainable conflict that generates panic; (2) the paralysis of the integrative functions of the Ego; (3) an attempt at Ego reorganization; (4) symptom formation, with the aim of avoiding to make direct contact with anguish, and (5) a pathological reorganization of the self, with a relative loss of the previous levels of Ego functioning. The consequence is a global functional deficit and lack of restitution of the premorbid personality.

Either for their constitutional Ego lability or for the reiteration of the crises, the patients who have suffered attacks of panic tending to a somatic discharge are more vulnerable to the trauma and to initiate regredient movements towards the body. According to the Freudian model of the actual neuroses, symptoms derive from the impossibility to elaborate the somatic sexual tension. The absence of psychic elaboration, of psychic meaning, brings the symptoms back to the sphere of the body. According to the Winnicottian model, a psychosomatic dissociation establishes itself. Once the panic crisis is produced, with its high Thanatotic charge and the effects of dissociation, subjects are in a state of regression and defencelessness similar to their first traumatic situation. There is a desperate search of an object that may allow them to bind all that Thanatotic charge. Thus they can look for a relative or a neighbour, an emergency room, or some psychoactive drug.

It may be inferred that in these cases, the mother was not able to contain and bind the original anguish and helplessness of her child. This was to the detriment of the acquisition of more evolved Ego defences and tended to the fixation of more primitive and extreme ones (turning against oneself, psychosomatic dissociation). The crisis of panic can also be understood as an attempt to repeat that state of unbearable inner tension that cannot be elaborated through representations in order to elaborate it and be able to bind it as a way to contain the Thanatotic invasion that threatens to annihilate the subject.

Anguish, anxiety

There is no doubt that panic is related to other less dramatic states, such as fear and dread, all of which are responses to dangerous situations. In this sense, there is also a very important relationship with anguish, which is a psychic response and an anticipatory signal of danger.

The clinical picture has been approached by several disciplines and catalogued as an "anxiety disorder" by psychiatric nosography (DSM V). It is quite frequent that people with intense anxiety fear to be imminently assaulted by the panic attack and consult as a result. Therefore, it is convenient to conceptually differentiate anxiety, anguish, and panic.

Because of their way of expressing themselves through symptoms, each of them has a certain predominance in the area in which they are manifested: anxiety in the sphere of behaviour and actions in the external world, anguish in the mental space, and panic in the body area. At the mental level, anxiety is registered like expectation and tension, with disagreeable nuances, propitiating varied acts of motor discharge that try to lighten the tension or to free themselves of it. Eating, smoking, talking, walking, sometimes working, etc., carried out all of them in excess, are an example. Their motives are usually conscious or preconscious for the subject. In all cases, there is an expectation of an uncertain outcome and the threat of a negative result or the fear of a loss, harm, or rejection linked to some significant test or desire (taking an exam, playing a crucial game, a love situation, work or economic outcomes, ups and downs of health conditions.) The subjects do not have the certainty of being able to resolve the situation or of having the means to bring about a favourable reassuring ending. This uneasiness (anxiety) may be caused by the fact that they have considered their available resources to be insufficient for this purpose or by the magnitude of the unfavourable conditions they will have to face.

In the field of psychoanalysis, Melanie Klein used the term "anxiety" to describe the processes that take place in the early stages of development, initially the schizoparanoid position and later the depressive one. Klein's theory abandons the scheme of libidinal phases and articulates anguish, defences, love, and aggression with the structuring of the object world. (In other psychoanalytical conceptualizations, the term anxiety is equivalent to anguish; their model is very different from the one we developed a few paragraphs ago in relation to discharge behaviours.)

Anxiety is a fundamentally psychical, mental experience. If we consider the psychic apparatus as a work machine, its task consists of binding undifferentiated energy so that it does not flow freely, mechanically, but linked to certain contents. On the other hand, this binding has as a correlate an inverse process of detachment or discharge, which is the liberation of raw energy. In this sense, it can be said that anguish is an unbinding or discharge phenomenon. The binding puts a brake on psychic and libidinal energy by means of representations and, perhaps, on a less elaborate level, by certain somatic reactions, which thus take on a meaningful value. This binding and elaboration also happen at different levels. At the lowest level, the problem of anguish and affect arises. "Whenever a physical sexual tension is abundantly generated but cannot become an affect by virtue of a psychical procedure, the sexual tension changes into anguish Affect itself is presented as one level of elaboration, a first level of binding, and anguish would mean the disorganization of affects or even the most elementary and primordial affect, close to an excitement that is discharged in an unspecified way. Affect is then a significant structure, but it does not mean that it needs representations to be qualified. Freud conceived of affect as being very close to the somatic: it is composed of an organized set of motor discharges (there is the binding, no doubt) added to a certain sensation of pleasure and/or displeasure. But it also has a historical aspect. Anguish is the less elaborated affect, the closest to a pure energetic discharge. However, it is amenable to a certain elaboration. It can be transformed into a meaningful element, into a sign" (Laplanche, 1981).

Freud maintains that anguish is, first and foremost, *felt*. We call it an affective state, although we do not truly know what an affect is. It is something, it is registered. It is not the result of something known (the subject's memory). It has bodily representatives (especially cardiac and respiratory). As something is felt, it needs the existence of an Ego capable of registering the sensation. If there is not an Ego yet, what is registered (felt) is rather the incapacity of the Ego to carry out such a registration. How can an affective state be registered when the conditions of binding are not yet available? In immature human offsprings, which depend on another individual, anguish would be an expression of uncertainty, of the confusion of someone who does not know what to do with his or her nostalgic structure; it is a reaction to the absence of an object.

How is anguish generated? It is generated as a reaction to a state of danger, and thereafter will regularly reproduce itself when such a state occurs again. If the traumatic situation is the experience of helplessness, anguish is, on the one hand, an expectation of the trauma and, on the other, a diminished repetition of it. Therefore, what turns anguish into neurosis is the replacement of the father for a horse (as in the case of Little Hans). In traumatic neuroses, anguish is not limited to the affect signal that sets the protective mechanisms in motion, but there is also the possibility of a reproduction of anguish by the economic conditions the traumatic situation generates. In general, anguish is involved in fundamental motor discharge innervations, and as is the case with all discharges, it follows certain paths in which there is an increase in excitation. For this reason, to establish those paths by circumventing the problem of representation, one resorts to the experience of birth. In this way, the problem of reproduction is solved too. It is the function of the Ego to reproduce anguish as an affective state for the purposes of defence. Affective states are included into the psychical life as sedimentations of ancient traumatic experiences, and in similar situations, they are awakened as mnemonic symbols.

The drive demands are not a danger in themselves because they entail a real external danger: castration. Thus, castration anguish is derived from another object and can be expressed by disfigurement (e.g., being bitten by a horse, eaten by a wolf, etc.). Anguish is a preparation for dealing with the quantity that bursts in.

We have already said that in terror there is no object, as there is in fear. Anguish protects against terror and against the terror neurosis. In terror there is no anguished preparedness either. This preparedness, with its overcathexis of the receptor systems, is the last barrier of the anti-stimulus shield. Fright (*schrek*) includes two combined elements: the lack of preparedness (a surprise factor) and the idea of an overflow (a concept already mentioned by Freud in the "Project of Psychology"). Scare is the triumph of the economic, of the quantitative force. Nothing has prepared the subjects for this overflow, they were not able to symbolize or pre-symbolize anything, they were not even alerted by a signal. There is no anguish either, and the Ego is dragged into a cataclysmic defence and begins to function just like a desire. There is an inner self-traumatic state that predisposes to fright: it is the hypnoid state, described in *Studies on Hysteria*; a state of division of fragmentation. Although the trauma is generated in two stages, the first do not prepare the subject for the second. There is a lack of preparedness and a paradox: fright continues to occur. The double overflow corresponds to a double scene. The notion of the sexual and the pre-sexual intervenes; it is only understood as a mutation in the capacity to symbolize. The sexual bursts into the pre-sexual stage, that is, into a state of unpreparedness to symbolize, is implanted in the Ego, is installed there, and is what determines the first scene. The second takes place a posteriori (in the case of sexuality, at puberty), and the subject begins to signify it by association. The role of the Ego, then, is to be surprised, attacked from within. There are indeed two times, but the first one does not prepare it for the other as a signal. The Ego is attacked against the grain; there is overflow, fright, and panic.

Even reduced to a minimum level, to its signal aspect, anguish should be enough to provoke a healthy reaction. But when it develops, when it is no longer just a signal but an anguished attack, it exceeds its objective. Turned into an attack, anguish is irrational, unmanageable. This is its pathological aspect. In the face of even a motivated anguish that develops and transforms itself into panic, we have reasons to search in the unconscious for something that echoes this panic and causes it. Thus, all real anguish, to the extent that it develops as such, must have an underlying neurotic anguish.

The external factors

The incidence of environmental factors in the predisposition to or triggering of panic situations can be understood from several viewpoints. We have already said that there is a sort of fashion in the current frequency of panic attacks, and it could be asked whether all the so-called ones correspond to this clinical picture or to diagnostic errors. On the other hand, the ways in which mental suffering is presented have been coloured by typical codes of these times, and in this way, new nosographies have appeared (new clothes for old pathologies), other clinical patterns have resurfaced or have increased. In the expression of panic attacks, the effect on the feeling of self, on the self itself, is crucial. On the outside, this feeling of self is supported by temporal and spatial continuities that allow the subjects to sustain their identity thanks to the recognition and appreciation of their family, social milieu, and work environment. Likewise, they are supported by belonging and inclusion in those environments, by their opportunity to participate in them, and by differentiation. Gilles Lipovetzky (1995), in his essays on contemporary individualism, states that the modern ideal of subordination of the individual to rational collective rules has been pulverized. This process of extreme personalization as a global strategy has produced a profound mutation in the doing and wanting of our societies, which has led to a postmodern society. In it, the indifference of the masses reigns, private autonomy is not discussed and nobody believes in the future anymore. "It has neither idols nor taboos, which introduces a discontinuity in the historical fabric. In that world where Narcissus has no solidarity networks, the subjectivity suffers from panic". In this dimension, panic is confronted with the disconnection of a representation established as an ideal. This kind of relationship with the ideal affects the subject. The Ego is a project for the future (Freud, "Introduction of narcissism"); it appears as a substitute for the ideal Ego. From its establishment, the subjective position is regulated by a symbolic reference that grants to the Ego its transcendence and is based on the unitary character of the Ego ideal. Its function as an insignia precipitates the identification of the ideal Ego. From then on, the experience of one's own Ego has the characters of unity in the present and of historical sameness.

Lacan has investigated the meaning structure in which the subject takes its place. At this point of the Ego ideal, subjects see themselves as the others see them; their identity is a function of the look of recognition of the other. There is a mirror, an imaginary look, an ideal, a symbolic look (para-identification), and the Ego ideal's function is to regulate this imaginary structure, the identifications, and conflicts arising in the Ego relations with fellow beings. When the support of the ideal disappears, when a sign that offered a witnessing gaze and sustained a project expires, symptoms are manifested. The Ego is updated in a stage of decomposition of its structure. When the social bond regulated by the ideal is broken, everything is possible, and this is reflected in fear of going crazy, of losing control – precisely what happens in panic.

Silvia Bleichmar (2005) states that "in our days the external environment becomes a scene where the demands and requirements of insertion, support and adaptation in order to survive put a strong pressure on the subjects and are the cause of intense discomfort, with repercussions in the social, family and work environments".

The ups and downs of all the above-mentioned factors are determining factors in the configuration of subjectivity. They promote processes of social dispersion and of subjective and bonding fragility and fragmentation, giving rise to numerous pathogenic symptoms and an intense mental suffering. The feelings of depersonalization, irritability, loss of motivation, and poor personal and work attainment are often translated into an inability to withstand any pressure. These conditions are imposed, in most cases, by demands for greater productive performance and provoke the fear of losing one's job, uncertainty, and instability.

In this area, working conditions can produce tiredness and fatigue, both physical and psychological, and these symptoms gradually translate into a feeling of "not being able to give more of oneself to others". Work stress establishes a lifestyle that progressively generates states of anguish, emotional exhaustion, disruptions in the rhythms of eating, physical activity, and rest. This tension or stress affects the mental and somatic defensive systems, reduces the defences and adaptive capacities of the subjects, and lowers their threshold of resistance to diseases. It generates experiences of insecurity, loss of control, and fantasies of destruction regardless of any effective danger. In short, this set of elements threatens with breaks and discontinuities in daily cohesion and stability, creating confusion, indecision, and ambiguity. The threat of a terminal disintegration affects the individual and collective dimensions of any project, and the sense and vision of the future are lost.

In addition, other codes and rules of our times also exert their effects. Many of them are linked to the incidence of globalization and mass communications. We are actors/spectators of a world where satellites, television, and computers bring the same images for all, the same information and the same fashions to distant and remote places on the planet. Catastrophic events, with their consequences of total annihilation and helplessness; sudden phenomena such as economic collapses (stock market crashes, currency depreciation, etc.); the danger of large-scale nuclear, chemical or bacteriological warfare, etc., are today experienced as an imminent threat by millions of people, many of whom suffer panic attacks. (Proof of this is that the current threat posed by COVID-19 pandemic has increased very much the number of consultations for panic symptoms or crises.) On the other hand, there is a trend towards uniformity and, at the opposite pole, an individualistic tendency that exacerbates differences among each people, each city, each human group, either peacefully or through the most extreme violence. Today, speed, immediacy, the flood of sensory stimuli, the primacy of market rules are the order of the day. Lenarduzzi (2005) lists the socio-cultural factors that increase general unhappiness:

A permanent need to adapt oneself to the fast transformations of the environment due to technological progress and the globalization policies of every nation.

The isolation that many people experience as a result of the loss of the support networks represented by the family, the neighbourhood, and the work environment.

The frequent migrations motivated by economic or labour reasons.

The increase in urban violence and the consequent lack of protection by the state.

The tension between the Ego and the Ideal Ego (the latter supported by the collective ideals of perfection and fortune advocated by the mass media).

The predominance of aesthetic models over ethical ones.

The distancing of human beings from themselves, which is expressed in a lesser dedication to reading, spirituality, and introspection.

The growing appreciation of the processes of discharge that provide immediate relief from any discomfort.

She suggests that the influence of these agents can be attributed to some morbid modalities of our time, such as addictions, anorexia, psychosomatic disorders, and panic. All of them are linked to the need to discharge sexual or aggressive tensions towards the body or the external world, as described by Freud when dealing with current neuroses.

The therapeutic situation

Patients who come to psychoanalytic treatment with all of the above characteristics have much trouble to "hook" (bind) with it. In consonance with the culture of our times, they peremptorily demand results – a symptomatic cure. They ask for something that, in principle, is beyond words and the talking cure. That is why they often come in search of psychiatric or psychopharmacological treatments. The need for the drug (mother) that calms and prevents their crises is the first agreement they will try to seal with their therapist. More than thinking, processing and elaborating, they will try to get magic solutions or proposals for resolving their difficulties.

A first stage usually includes the prescription of psychotropic drugs, which in case of mitigating their crises, will promote in them a certain level of confidence – a necessary basis to link them to the treatment and make them believe in the possibility of being heard, understood, and relieved. In spite of this, their need to discharge "in short circuit", attributable to failures in the organization of the preconscious (Marty, 1992) or to overflows of it due to environmental traumas, puts a strong pressure in achieving "results" that may calm and reassure them.

Therefore, several authors suggest that to cope with distress it is essential to enhance the patient's feelings of control, predictability, and resources (Sandler J.) or to focus selectively on the analysis of both the sources or causes of distress and the subjects' reaction to it (Hugo. Bleichmar, 2016).

When causes are placated, the affluence and flow of anxiety are reduced. But this is not enough. It is extremely important to enhance the confidence in the therapist and his/her methods so that patients do not keep themselves at a distance, feel insecure or suffer a regression. Patients feel that their neurovegetative system has been "primed" like a weapon and is ready to be used against them. The repetition of the crisis causes them to fear its reappearance and shakes their feelings of power, of basic security, of trust in their body and mind, and in their ability to self-regulate. Both the exterior and the interior become a source of fear and of potential attacks. Many do not even know when or how they will suffer, in an abrupt and traumatic way, the assault of these intolerable experiences, before which they feel absolutely helpless and defenceless.

The first crisis is usually intensely remembered and operates, in the patients' mind, as a traumatic event that shakes their narcissism in a way equivalent to an unhappy love affair or the experience of post-traumatic stress. There is a before-and-after the event that leaves them "marked" with the imprint of vulnerability. That first crisis is usually unique and unleashes in a special way for each patient. However, what happens next is universal: all patients feel that their body and mind have stopped functioning in the normal way.

The first stage of the treatment must confront this state of disarticulation and defencelessness, the regression and the need for magical, fusional, and idealized dependence of an all-protective bond, with other situations in which precisely the paranoid defences against such need were manifested. These are difficult moments: it is necessary to make the patients "nest", find a space where their very primitive anxieties, such as the fear of collapse (of disintegrating, of falling indefinitely) may be contained. There is a need of a maternal holding equivalent to that of the baby's stage of absolute dependence. Bolognini (2010) affirms that "in the initial phase of treatment with these patients, there is a fusional effect that brings them relief and well-being, but even small discontinuities in the setting (the weekend separation) or in the dialogue (not immediate confirmations) are enough to cancel a symptomatic benefit that could not be sustained and turned into an effective structural change". If they go ahead, they establish strongly idealized transferences, with a magical oral dependence on the analyst – such that they need to communicate with him or her in the intervals between sessions "to hear his/her voice" and so feel more protected.

Celia (26 years old, two young daughters, a teacher) stated it in this way: "In the early days of my treatment, coming here or listening to you [the therapist] was like a drug for me". Celia began her crisis shortly after the birth of her second daughter. She wanted a boy. Much later, she was able to verbally express her homicidal desires regarding this daughter. When she was a child, her father left her wife and daughter prematurely after divorcing and she was raised by an all-knowing intruder mother, who continued to transmit her "wisdom" and disqualify her "for her own good" until today.

Some of the most relevant difficulties in these treatments tend to be the almost intolerable dependence on the analyst with the simultaneous enactment of aggression in the process, basically with attacks against the setting. If overcome, these situations allow to put the archaic traumatic into words. On the other hand, the use of psychosomatic dissociation as a frequent defence leads patients to resort to several doctors in their crises, receiving varied and sometimes contradictory indications, which complicate the psychoanalyst's work. The organization of a clinical-psychopharmacological "support team" usually helps in this case. It works as a wide net that increases the available resources since the lateral transferences add members capable of providing confidence and security to the patients while reducing their demands on a single figure. In this way, the personnel of an emergency room, a general physician, a psychopharmacologist, some family members, neighbours or friends can serve as "protective/tranquilizing objects" that, articulated together with the psychotherapist, allow to go around the attacks in this stage.

These treatments are usually carried out in several phases. For some authors, this implies gradually increasing the feeling of control, working with the triggering conflicts and the reaction to the anguish, with what was experienced and felt as dangerous, as well as with the subject's beliefs about being unable to tolerate the anguish since they feel it grows supposedly unlimited. Difficulties in the capacity to symbolize, together with the strong psycho-soma dissociation and the absence of an organic memory of the traumatic moments, lead very often to an elaborate process of remembering and reconstruction. The weak Ego constitution, which gives rise to defensive mechanisms and a false self, indicates, in turn, a distortion in the dynamics that is at the core of object interaction; thus, there is a tendency to introjective difficulties and "incorporative concealment" (Grinberg, 1990). All this makes patients to cling with oral anxiety and magical expectations to drugs, which are never entirely tranquilizing. In fact, the temporary fusion with the analyst is only partially reassuring.

We must also deal with the hard experience, projected into the future, of an endless oral dependence on protective objects, since after the crises, patients consider that they cannot be trusted to solve by themselves the difficulties that arise. Its opposite is the yearning of a *restitutio ad integrum*, of a strong and secure Ego, like the one the subject had before the crisis. When symbolization is already possible, other aspects of the psychosomatic vulnerability appear: the false adaptive self, excessive demands of the ideal Ego, Oedipal and castration fantasies, suffocation of aggressiveness, and its discharge in the body under the form of self-attacks.

A desirable achievement of the treatment would be that patients could feel confidence in themselves and, as part of that process, tolerate the separation from the analyst without being crashed. This would imply recognizing one's own self with its positive and negative aspects, to make contact with one's grief, to articulate one's history without resorting to denial or defensiveness as extreme resources, to go through experiences of letting oneself float, lose, etc., with body and mind, without fear and without the need for control. "To appropriate a more relaxed and competent self, which 'lets live' – writes Bolognini –. To fluctuate with pleasure in areas of preconscious mental life, immersing and emerging between the primary and the secondary processes without feeling too much fear. The search for a long-awaited authenticity, a treaded separation and a sufficient harmony between the elements of the inner world becomes the true evolutionary achievement of the subject" (Bolognini, *ibid.*).

From another viewpoint, the anguish of separation, the aggressiveness and its consequences, the feeling of guilt and persecution need a careful working-through. The sources of the narcissistic disorder, the oppression imposed to the development of the self by the significant others, and the loss of the sensation of being an active agent of one's own life, etc., must be thoroughly investigated. All this reduces the conditions that may set off the circuits of anguish.

Bibliography

Baranger M, Personal communication.

Baranger, W y M, Mom J (1987) "El trauma psíquico infantil de nosotros a Freud, Revista de Psicoanálisis, Tomo XLIV N° 4 APA.

Baumgart A. (2010) *Ataque de pánico y subjetividad*. Buenos Aires: Eudeba.

Bion (1984) *Learning from experience*. London: Routledge.

Bleichmar, H. (2016) Trastorno de pánico: aplicación del enfoque modular transformacional a la comprensión de su patología y tratamiento, en De pánicos y furias, la clínica del desborde, Lugar Editorial.

Bleichmar, S. (2005) *La subjetividad en riesgo*. Buenos Aires: Topia Editorial.

Bolognini, S. (2010) Secret passages, the theorie and technique of interpsychic relations, The new library of Psychoanalysis.

Busch, F.N., Shear, M.K., Cooper, A.M., Shapiro, R., y Leon, A. (1995) 'An empirical study of defense mechanisms in panic disorders', *Journal of Nervous and Mental Disorders*, 183, pp. 299–303.

De Masi, F. (2004) 'The psychodynamic of panic attacks: A useful integration of psychoanalysis and neurosciences', *International Journal of Psychoanalysis*, 85, pp. 311–336.

Diamond, D.B. (1985) 'Panic attacks, hypochondriasis and agoraphobia: A self psychology formulation', *American Journal of Psychotherapy*, 39, pp. 114–125.

Dsm, V. *Diagnostic and statistical manual of mental disorders*. American Psychiatric Association. 2013, AMP is the author

Ferro, A. (1996) 'Carla's panic attacks, insight and transformation', *International Journal of Psychoanalysis*, 77, pp. 997–1011.

Freud, S., Breuer, J. (1895) *Studies on hysteria, standard edition vol II*.

"(1914'16) On Narcissism, Standard Edition vol XIV.

"(1915) Drives and Their Vicisitudes, Standard Edition vol XIV.

"(1917) The Uncanny, Standard Edition vol XVII.

"(1921) Group psychology and the Analysis of the Ego, Standard Edition vol XVIII.

"(1926) Inhibitions Symptoms and Anxiety, Standard Edition vol XX.

"(1937) Analysis Terminable and Interminable, Standard Edition vol XXIII.

Green, A. (1986) *Life narcissism, death narcissism*. London: Free Association Books.

Green, A. (1999) *The work of the negative*. London: Free Association Books.

Greenson, R.R. (1959) 'Phobia, Anxiety, and Depression', *Journal of the American Psychoanalytic Association*, 7, pp. 663–674.

Grinberg, L. (1990) *The goals of psychoanalysis, identification, identity and supervision*. London: Karnac Books.

Klein, M. (1975) *Complete works of Melanie Klein*. S Lawrence: Delacorte Press.

Kohut, H. (1971) *The Analysis of the Self*. Chicago, London: The University of Chicago Press.

Laplanche, J. (1981) *La angustia*. AE: Buenos Aires.

Lenarduzzi, H. (2005) 'El ataque de pánico, una perspectiva integradora', *Psicosomática: aportes teóricos-clínicos en el siglo XXI*. Buenos Aires, Lugar.

Lipovetzky, G. (1995) *The Ephemeral Era*. Johns Hopkins University Press.

Mahler, M. (2000) *The psychological birth of the human infant, symbiosis and individuation*. Basic Books (Copyright Year 1975), Published December 31, 1985 by Routledge.

Marty P. (1992) Psicosomática del adulto AE. Amorrotu Editores

Pao, P.N. (1979) *Schizofrenic disorders*. Nueva York: International University Press.

Rubinstein, R., y Bichi, E (1997) 'Cibersexo, Vigencia del Psicoanálisis en nuestra cultura', *40° Congreso Internacional de Psicoanálisis*. Barcelona. Revista Asociación Psicoanalitica Argentina, 1998 vol 55 n 3

Rubinstein, R, y D'Arriaga, J. (1993) 'Ser o no ser, Psicosomático es la cuestión', *Monografia en APA*.

Sandler, J. (1987) *From safety to superego*. London: Karnac.

Saurí, J. (1979) *Las fobias*. Buenos Aires: Nueva Visión.

Vangaard, T. (1989) *Panic: The course of psychoanalysis.* Nueva York: Norton.

Winicott, D. (1988) 'Mind and Its Relation with the Psyche Soma', in *Human Nature*, Brunner Mazel Ed.

Chapter 2

Danger erotization, adventure, and addiction to adrenaline

We increasingly observe the presentation of symptomatic and character-ologic subjects who erotically charge the situations of danger or risk and, concomitantly, become addicted to the adrenalinic effects of these situations and their experience or their overcoming of it. Likewise, the supply and social consumption of certain sport activities, risk sports, and expeditions or adventures in natural environments with increasing danger have expanded as a temporary and limited mode of experience. Knowing the particularities of the erogenous will allow us to deepen our understanding of these phenomena.

Based on Freud's exposition in "Three Essays on the Theory of Sexuality" (1905), we observe that what will afterwards become erogenous is generated in a source, encompasses specific zones of the body, and is determined by certain conditions of the stimulus. With respect to the source, "sexual excitement is born as a carbon copy of a satisfaction experienced as a result of other organic processes" Both the stimulus and certain erogenous areas of the body are capable of arousing feelings of pleasure. However, the quality of the stimulus is considered more important than the characteristics of the body areas, and the regular or periodic character of the stimulus is as significant as its intensity. These areas can be a sector of skin or mucosa in which stimulations of a certain kind cause a pleasant sensation of a certain quality. There are pre-determined erogenous zones, as shown by sucking, a model of autoeroticism in which children do not use a foreign object but rather a part of their own skin because it is more convenient, since in this way, they become independent from the external world which they cannot yet dominate, and then seek a second erogenous zone, although of lesser value. Any other sector of the skin or mucous membranes can provide the services of an erogenous zone, although it must meet certain conditions. As with sucking, any sector of the body can have the excitability of the genitals and be elevated to the condition of an erogenous zone. This property can be permanently attached to certain parts of the body and also possibly encompass all internal organs.

DOI: 10.4324/9781003293569-3

Even the displeasing can become an erogenous source. For example, the effect of sexual excitement of many affects that are in themselves displeasing, such as anguish, fearful trembling, or fright, is preserved in a great number of human beings during their adult life and explains why many people wait for the opportunity to receive such sensations, subject only to some concomitant circumstances (their belonging to a world of fiction, writing or theatre) that diminish the intensity of the displeasure.

The sensations of intense pain provoke an identical erogenous effect, especially when the pain is diminished by a concomitant condition. This relationship is one of the roots of the sadomasochistic impulse.

Other times sexual excitement is generated as a side effect of a large series of internal processes, for which it is enough that the intensity of the latter (the intensity of the stimulus as quantitative factor) exceeds certain thresholds. This excess can be a determining factor added to the significant imprint of the stimulus. Perhaps nothing of certain importance occurs in the organism that does not yield its components to the excitation of the sexual drive. This libidinous coexcitation caused by a painful and displeasing tension is likely to be a childish physiological mechanism that is later exhausted. All this is associated with masochism, both the erogenous (pleasure of receiving pain) and the moral and feminine one.

For A. Green, at the beginning of life, there is a link between sexuality and pain in the name of libidinal coexistence. This gives rise to a certain form of pleasure: masochism. One can thus speak of something that is "beyond the principle of pleasure-displeasure" as a matrix, where pleasure and displeasure are not separated. Only in the eyes of the other does displeasure appear as a negative pleasure; for the subject, there is a mixed sensation that is neither pleasant nor displeasing: a coexcitation that could perhaps be defined as "tension intensity". One could even speak of something that is beyond displeasure, helplessness, unhappiness, conjured up by a kind of sensation, and amalgamated. In the severe neuroses, the neuroses of character, the narcissistic structures, and the borderline cases, one can attest to the validity of non-intricate forms of destructiveness, which are between the life drive and the death drive. In all these cases, we may assume that the dominant mechanism is a mourning impossible to overcome, together with the defensive reactions that this gives rise to.

These concepts can be articulated with the processes that give an erogenous quality to danger and adventure. To what Freud suggested in 1905 as a source (the organic processes), we add today the knowledge of the humoral chemical mechanisms activated during physical exercise in general and in risky situations in particular. At a central, autonomic, and endocrine level, the nervous system secretes endorphins and catecholamines (the fear hormones, which affect almost all organs and functions: the nervous, circulatory and digestive systems, the musculature, and the cerebral function). Their effects translate into a sharpening of the senses, a decrease in pain, and pleasurable and euphoric sensations. On the other hand, fear associated with danger of life, loss of fortune, etc., arouses another aspect of erogeneity (as we said about fear and fright). In turn, the quantitative factor, the intensity of the stimulus (in this case, the implicit risk), causes a "marginal effect", a "collateral excitation" with a high quantum of erogeneity. This is similar to what happens with pain insofar as the individual manages to diminish it or circumvent it by passing the physical tests and demands.

Pleasure, adventure, sport

In recent years we have witnessed the flourishing and development of sport practices whose distinctive mark is to run risks and have adventures in natural environments. Their supply and growing consumption have gone hand in hand with the benefits they bring to the tourism, clothing, and equipment industries. Many of these practices derive from classic sports. What is new and remarkable about "adventure sport" is that, whether in a free or organized way, it puts the subject in contact with nature.

The objective of its practitioners is to overcome the obstacles presented by certain natural elements, such as water, mountains, snow, air, and at the same time to overcome themselves. There is an intrinsic pleasure generated by the activity itself, to which is added a sense of challenge and achievement. For this, it is necessary to develop, sometimes very rigorously, physical qualities and capacities, motor skills, great general resistance, and, most importantly, a psychological preparation. No less important is the need for teamwork as well as cooperation and synchronization between disciplines. In these sports, it is crucial to know how to orient oneself: where one stands, where one should point to, and how to move in an unknown terrain where nature imposes its rules. Also to be highlighted as one of the attractive and stimulating vectors of these sports is the uncertainty created by the environment, making them different from those more regulated and practiced in more limited spaces.

The adventure sports can be classified in those that are practiced in the mountains (such as climbing, canyoneering or rappelling, mountain cycling and riding, etc.), those that are carried out in water (canoe or kayak descent, rafting, canoeing, diving, kitesurfing) and those in air (bungee jumping, parachuting, hang gliding, paragliding, zip-lining, etc.).

On the other hand, there are resistance sports, which require great physical and psychological effort due to the amount of time they take and the distance to be covered, being a true test of self-sufficiency for those who practice them; and the so-called "explosive" ones because they generate intense sensorial experiences in a short period of time, producing a hormonal and chemical shock, with its consequent pleasure and well-being. There are mixed varieties or those that combine sport and athletics with tourism (trekking in diverse terrains, marathons, triathlons and mixed tests, etc.).

In the United States, risk sport activities are grouped under the name of "extreme games", which since the mid-1990s have gathered crowds at annual festivals. However, the lack of an agglutinating federative body on a global level has led to organizational dispersion and has made it difficult to classify the activities according to the place where different risky practices are carried out. An enormous amount of names are used to refer to these risky activities or sports: adventure sports, extreme sports, active tourism, etc. Due to their dynamic evolution, one or another name is used to highlight different aspects of this type of sports.

A set of captivating experiences and sensations have been pointed out as their main appeal for the participants, namely:

- The break with the codes and routines of everyday life in order to settle oneself in the midst of novelty, uncertainty, and danger offers channels to drive release and satisfaction. This discharge is well accepted by the Ego. Here the subject must not confront an instinctual inner danger but rather the elements of nature (air, mountain, water). When confronting a natural danger (often mortal), individuals can get rid of their anguish of death and castration, placing in the exterior the threatening, violent forces with which they must deal – forces that may represent their Superego. There is not here a fight between the Ego and its impulses, but between the Ego and the external world, as it happened in the beginnings of the structuring of the psyche. By loosening the mechanisms of repression, this free expression and discharge of the drive and aggressiveness have as a correlate a strong pleasant effect.
- The challenge, the defiance, and the confrontation have an important role. When practicing these sports, many athletes and players are faced with demands in which they test their own competence. In these cases, the pleasure of competition refers to the fight with an Oedipal, fraternal, or similar rival.
- When dealing with challenges presented by nature, overcoming the risky situations leads to experiencing a strong feeling of self-assertion and power, along with relief from the disappearance of danger. Some individuals refer to it as an intoxicating, quasi-orgasmic experience. They feel themselves as in a sort of manic position, full of omnipotence. By confronting and defeating the forces of nature and destiny, helplessness, suffering, and neurotic misery are apparently reversed. It is like defeating an archaic and sadistic Superego, the product of primitive introjections of feared parental figures, to be less exposed to their Tanathotic effects through a delusionary demonstration of strength, talent, and skill, or intuition. In this context, the aim is also to find a limit, a cut, a mark, which can appear in the form of a serious accident and even death. The possibility of suffering an accident is always present, and perhaps it is part of that quantum of excitement and risk that gives the activity its particular character.

The deployment of aptitudes and Ego functions in the overcoming of these tests – instead of the neurotic, psychotic or perverse symptoms that leave their stamp of impossibility and limitation– makes the potential anguishing and helplessness feelings change into pleasant and powerful ones. In the so-called risk professions (soldiers, Formula 1 pilots, war correspondents, etc.), these constellations can become part of the subject's character or of his/her normal way of life.

The manifestations of the castration complex, either as a way of compensating feelings of inferiority or in the testing of "what I can-what I can't", with the Oedipal suggestion of being phallic/being castrated, are associated with some other ones helpful for those who need to reestablish their narcissistic balance, their feelings of worth and self-esteem. All of them find here a fertile though the steep path to achieve such purposes. Of course, to this end, each type of adventure will offer a variable degree of risk.

The search for new and vivifying sensations, coupled with experiences of purity (breathing pure air, drinking fresh and clean water in waterfalls or in mountain streams) and the sense of freedom in the immensity of nature, the fact of feeling the freshness of the wind in the heights, of the sun and vegetation without pollution, of jungles and wild forests: all this counteracts states of anguish, oppression, and confinement. The autoerotic and sensory stimulation not only conjures up these states but also reestablish the narcissistic balance based on the body and the senses, all of which is fundamental for feeling oneself. The more an individual is challenged and threatened by conflicts of various kinds, the more he or she finds here an outlet and an energetic and stimulating toning up. On the other hand, some individuals (such as teenagers who drive cars or motorcycles at high speed, those who practice bungee jumping on their graduation trips, etc.) face through these activities identity problems.

It is useful to compare these practices with ordinary sports. During a common sport activity, the movement, the game, and the competition are sources of pleasure and of drive discharge and satisfaction in a scenario in which the objective reality is partially denied and relegated by the kind of environment and the rules of the game. There is an intense object bonding and commitment (imposed by the competition) with people who are the targets of the aggressive discharges.

Those who practice adventure sports tend to be more confrontational with themselves and with nature and are more exposed to the effects of drive defusion and disengagement. This could be attributed to the scarce or null participation of the playful component. Play, being in an intermediate condition between the inner world and reality (Winnicott, 1971), allows in greater measure the unfolding of fantasy and the displacement or personification of aspects of the internal world in the objects that individuals have at their disposal on the outside (the other players). It also lends itself to channelling, discharging, and linking sadism to those objects.

A clinical vignette

Matías comes to the consultation moved by the death of two close friends in the last 15 months. At the beginning of the first interview, he shakes my hand firmly, holding on, while he exclaims, as if with relief: "I've finally found you!" Then he says that he had been seeing a therapist irregularly for the last two years but had long since noticed a stagnation in the process.

"I was told that you were going to hit the button with what was happening to me", says M. "What is described in your article I read in Internet is an echo of my life. I need to do extreme things to feel alive, stimulated. To run with the car at 200 km per hour, even if it rains; or to glide down off the top of a mountain. Once I traveled to a foreign country and threw myself into an abyss; most of the other boys, when were about to reach the edge, slowed down a bit, had a kind of shock. I continued on and felt a lot of pleasure in doing so, I almost laughed. This is the omnipotent attitude you referred to in the article, the desire for death, the search for limits. I understand that it is what I do, but I don't know why. That's why I come here. During the time I was in treatment, I managed to reduce a bit my level of exposure to risk. Now I'm calmer about it, but I'm haunted by a very intense distress. And I don't want to feel bad. Nevertheless, when I act like this, I feel good with myself".

Matías is alarmed by the death of two of his close friends, who were very similar to him. "We liked the same things, the same carefree way of living, the same passion", he adds. He repeats once and again that he wants to stop in time, not to have a bad end. We agreed to do a few weekly interviews and then start the treatment properly.

Matías is 45 years old, he has been married for eight years and has four children; the first three are 7, 5, and 3 years old, and the fourth one is 18 months old. He has a comfortable economic situation, a product of his work and many "fortune's strikes", as he says.

He went through several turns of fortune over time, alternating very intense hardships and sublime, lively moments. "I touched the sky with my hands and changed the tin into gold", he says, "feeling that everything I wanted was within my reach". His boastful and provocative tone contrasts with the enormous anxiety that consumes him, that leads him to spend whole days crying without knowing why when he "stops the machine".

Matías is well aware that a good part of his behaviour has its origin in childhood experiences. He is the penultimate of a very large series of nine siblings who lived in a religious-mystical environment with strong prejudices against abortion; he assumes that he was an unwanted child. "We should not have had you, you are a Judas in skin, a rebel, a traitor, a bastard":

sentences like these have been painfully anchored in his soul. "I did not make so much trouble, nor was I so rebellious", he comments. "The truth is that they had little or no patience with me, no dedication, hardly gave me food and clothes".

His father was a rural teacher who at home had (in Matías' words) a distant, dictatorial, and punishing behaviour: he shouted a lot, lashed with a whip, and imposed penances. His mother also mistreated him; she was a cold woman who demanded him to fulfil his duties and tasks, permanently distrusted him and controlled that his reactions did not go out of the mould. Her main interest was that everything be neat, orderly and ready so that her husband would not get angry.

At the age of 13, Matias frees himself from this environment by going to study in a nearby town; he spends weekends at the house of an uncle and an aunt, old and lonely but good-tempered people for whom his visits were a breath of air. "It was hard, but they treated me better than at home", he says. At least there he knew quite well what he could expect, since the system of rewards and punishments was clear. He remembers being an excellent student, the best in his class for several years. "It was always clear to me that I had to do my best, give myself entirely to achieve my goals, to be recognized, to be important to others".

After graduating from high school, he begins to work and pay for his studies in order to stay in college, where he learns Agricultural Administration. He also meets what he calls "the love of his life": Florence. Their common history is marked with the fate of the impossible. Rarely could they find or develop a viable common project, as external interferences (other couples, jobs of both of them) would get in the way every time they tried. He misses now the encounters with Florence, which impacted him beyond the sexual level: it could be simply a chat, a walk, a look, suddenly going together to a church and feeling that they were elevated by the holy music, the aromas, the climate. These experiences had a mystical character, like an ecstasy, which (as happened with his risky experiences) made him feel the adrenaline running through his veins and turning him alive.

Matías incessantly asks himself about the reasons for his behaviour and his emotional states. The desire and permanent fear of losing Florence, their repeated separations, were intolerable to him and plunged him into states of anguish, abandonment, and loneliness. In the sessions, we tried to build bridges between these Ego-dissociated, split states.

A. (ANALYST): What do you feel is the role your wife, your children, your home play in your feelings of loneliness and abandonment?

M. (MATÍAS): They are what is stable, what is secure. I love them, but what I feel with Florencia is different, touches me at another place, I don't have words to explain it.

He also lacks words to describe his frantic need of risky actions. He is like a drug addict who tries to reduce and graduate the dose because he is aware that unrestraint may lead him to inexorable death; nevertheless, he defies death again and again. When he "wins", he feels triumphant and omnipotent: he is then the "boss", the chief, the one admired, who can do everything.

After three months of treatment, a transferential bond is established with idealized and persecutory nuances. He needs me, flatters me, and fears me:

M.: I have never been understood with such precision and depth by anybody. With you I can talk about everything I feel without keeping anything to myself, just as I am. I wouldn't want you to take away my pleasure in running at high speed in the car, gambling or having fun with women. I wouldn't want to fall into sadness, loneliness and depression. I want to avoid it. I'm here to feel better and take fewer risks. I don't want to go through a severe downturn.

A.: You hope that I will help you contain and sustain those painful affects that you can't connect with at present, and that you need to run away from with all the drugs you already know. You fear me because you believe that I may let you exposed, with no support, as when you were a child.

The memories of his earliest childhood are a stumbling block that he cannot yet overcome. He tells me of the punishments and neglect I mentioned above and of the affection, respect, and care in the way he treats people, friends, and clients, but especially of the reparation-intended actions, he takes with disadvantaged people (tramps, prostitutes, unrecoverable addicts).

In a session, I ask him if he thinks he could be loved if he were nothing else but himself, and he quickly answers: "My children love me". To which I point out that even there, he places himself in the position of an affection-giver and does not express his needs but denies them.

The early traumas, the unrepresentable trace of that love that did not exist, covered with acts and impulses, beat him every time he needs an adrenaline discharge to counteract the derivatives of those primary affections.

As happens with perversions, that extra pleasure covering the traumatic – that plus where danger threatens to phagocyte the essence of his being– remains eroticized in Matías, and he recognizes himself as its prisoner. The joy that adrenaline brings with it covers the experience of emptiness, perhaps of not being (wanted, desired). At a certain moment of the therapeutic process, it was only possible to mention such experiences cursorily. Vertigo monopolized his feelings and the way he felt himself.

The transference reveals his longing to be saved and redeemed, as he saves and redeems unhappy or disadvantaged people. His early resistances to the treatment, in the form of absences to sessions for reasons of work or through the intellectualized understanding of his conflicts, seem to be defensive mechanisms that he uses to regulate the contact in the transference with affective states, which he then felt intolerable.

Matías currently feels that the quantum of anguish has been decreasing, that the questions without immediate answers can be more "nested" in him, the same that they are "nested" in the treatment (Bichi, 2003). He sporting-like reserves for himself a lower dose of adrenaline, speeding up a bit from time to time or sending text messages to Florence to feel that she is present (with him).

Adrenaline addiction

Is it legitimate to think of an adrenaline addiction?

Strictly speaking, adrenaline is a substance secreted by the adrenal glands as part of the body's response to a dangerous situation. All of its effects on various organs and systems are intended to prepare them to respond in the best possible way to the demands some activity puts on the body. In this way, it favours glycolysis (glucose release) so that the individual is ready for a likely rise in consumption, augments the frequency and contractions of the heart, dilates the bronchi, increases the irrigation and contractility of the skeletal muscles (for actions such as running), dilates the pupils (for better vision), decreases the time of blood clotting, etc. Adrenaline intervention is not reduced exclusively to physical efforts or to the practice of adventure sports. It is also secreted in a typical love encounter or in an incident of verbal aggression. The effects of this substance are blushing, hands and lips trembling, palpitations, or the sensation of having a knot in the stomach. It also stimulates the brain production of dopamine, associated with the cerebral system of pleasure, which generates the feelings of joy and reinforcement that motivates a person proactively to perform certain activities. It participates in naturally gratifying experiences such as eating and sex, those linked to the use of some addictive substances, and the neutral stimuli associated to all this.

Both adrenaline and dopamine are secreted in the practice of risk sports. They are two of the hormones included in the group of catecholamines, which function as neurotransmitters in the central nervous system. They fulfil different functions, though directly interrelated. In adventure sports, these two hormones play fundamental roles. On the one hand, adrenaline prepares the organism, psychically and physiologically, for situations of "danger" or "risk"; in addition, it stimulates the production of dopamine. The latter is in charge of making the individuals feel pleasure and joy so that they want to perform the activity again.

It has long been known that when strong physical activities are carried out, the brain produces a great amount of substances called endorphins. Their main action is to block the brain detectors of pain (which are found in the brain and midbrain) to produce analgesia. Interestingly, endorphins are closely related to the release of ACTH, one of the hormones released during stress.

What is the influence of adrenaline and dopamine in risk sports? Despite having different physiological effects, they manifest subjectively according to the intensity of the activity and the emotion it conveys. The effect can be momentary and of high impact or prolonged and sustained; endorphins have a short life in the body, as they are eliminated to keep it balanced. If they circulated freely through it, we would feel no pain whatsoever, and pain is the only way to realize that we have some physical problem. Physical exercise, especially of the resistance kind (running, walking on a mountain, riding a bicycle, swimming), stimulate the production of endorphins.

To this stimulating biological effect must be added the psychic component of pleasure obtained from the discharge and release of tension through the muscular apparatus. Concomitantly, the relief, the sensation of triumph, and aggrandizement of the Ego for overcoming risks also contribute their share in obtaining pleasure and well-being. By these means, the search of risky situations and their overcoming become necessary to eliminate or suppress experiences of pain, anguish, or emptiness unbearable for the subject.

We speak of addiction when urgent impulses are imposed periodically or regularly on subjects like Matías and lead them to look for something in the external world or to carry out actions that, due to their mental and biological consequences, upset their affective and mental state, as happens with drug addicts. We assume that their psychic apparatus is incapable of processing increases in tension since the anti-stimulus barrier has been altered. No binding processes or representational mediation allow another route of derivation. The urgency to get rid of the unbearable pain, that cannot find words to express it or calm it, is evacuated through action, but with the cost of emotional suppression and the always present possibility of annihilation of the subject.

The traumatic experience and its repetition remain as parts of a split unconscious, barren of representations and bonds, but fertile as regards the effect of the Nirvana principle, in the expectation that the acts performed will remove any state of tension, pain, and even desire.

Another clinical vignette

Going back to Matías, we wonder if it is only the eroticization of danger that leads him to take frequent risks. Does he do these things because of his need to challenge somebody and, at the same time, to look for limits or a Law framing him? Or perhaps the most unrestrained Tanathotic impulse is what leads him to play, to flirt again and again with death until he finds it?

The analogy and differences with another patient, Tomás – a 62-year-old economist with many years of psychoanalytical treatment, unhappy in his marriage with three young children – may shed light on this.

Tomás belongs to the second generation of Asian immigrants, with part of his family dismembered, and suffers from the indifference of his parents, who are involved in a massive mourning process. New detachments due to labour issues and the fear of hunger, poverty, and even the danger of a war conflagration led this family to migrate to Argentina more than 50 years ago.

I will only mention the last significant events in their lives. Their two eldest children are getting ready to emancipate and go to live on their own. Tomás is almost determined to initiate a divorce, and an occasional meeting with a cousin makes him relive with intensity a part of the family history before his birth, full of secrets and twists of fate – family members killed in purges, scams, jail, other migrations.

Tomás decides to take a vacation to bid farewell (to his children?) by hiring a risky tour crossing the Andean Mountains. This adventure was extremely dangerous: countless cliffs, strong wind, cold weather, the need to cross places full of ice, etc., added to his lack of training.

He returns from that trip exultant, very energized and vital, almost euphoric because of the purity of air at those heights, the healthy effect of natural life, the difficulties he overcame, and the renewed communication with his children. He underlines the "sensory experience" and the stimulant, "adrenalinic" effect of his feat. However, the search for risk, which could have cost him his life, is firmly and omnipotently denied by Tomás, possibly as a result of the lot of losses that he suffered, still suffer and will always suffer, which he is still unable to metabolize psychically.

In its origin, as A. Green (1999) writes, the typical manifestation of the death drive destructivity is decathexis. And in its de-objectivizing function, far from being confused with mourning, it becomes the most radical opposition to the work of mourning, which is central to the transformation processes characteristic of the objectifying function.

Both Tomás and Matías know what is happening to them, but they are not capable of thinking it through by giving these situations representability (Botella and Botella, 2004). It is as if what happens to them takes place in a "psychic-prepsychic zone situated on either side of the world of representations, especially that of the word-representations, of preconscious formations, of rationality". Its existence is part of the unconscious life but is not assimilated into the Unconscious system, which, as defined by Freud, is composed of repressed representations. These are events that have not achieved the state of representability – if one considers psychic functioning as a permanent work of representation.

According to Botella, the idea of a "non-inscription" since a trauma took place in childhood revolutionizes the notions of memory and of memory trace. This author affirms that in severely disturbed patients, there is a "memory without remembrance", which would correspond to the negative of the trauma and the traumatic experience before the acquisition of language and the capacity to inscribe memory traces.

Based on Bion's model, and in particular, on his notion of alpha function, he suggests that memory without remembrances does not meet the necessary condition to be transformed into represented memory and incorporated into a story. "It remains in a pre-psychic rather than psychic state, a state of non-remembering, waiting for an element that, by transforming its nature, will allow it to access representation and consciousness. We could say that this memory without remembrances is a kind of negative process, which can only manifest itself as a 'hole', a 'psychic void' in the fabric of representations. But it may acquire other qualities that are not those of representation. For example, in analytical practice we find it under its sensory or even frankly hallucinatory aspect, also in the form of an act, of behavior".

In both Matías and Tomás, these acts are deceptively masked by the intoxicating and overwhelming experience of the adventure, with all the particularities and nuances we have exposed. Their repetitive character reveals "that which cannot be integrated into a chain of representations, into a story, transformed into a tale. It is like something invisible, a sort of sketch, a potential script that silently determines psychic life, without being directly manifested, not even by means of substitutes: a 'defect of thought' that shows the limitations of words to describe unconscious processes".

The work of representability, by making something intelligible, responds to the Freudian definition of linking, one of the earliest and most important functions. It represents the hidden side of psychic intelligibility.

They preserve untransformed states of existence in the manner of Bion's (1963) beta particles. They are like psychic fragments that push or press in doing and not in remembering or evoking; they have a way of bursting in like proto-memories, as primary symbolizations, not transformed yet into memories, temporarily united to those affects that are part of these elementary systems.

But what differentiates Tomás, as well as many other occasional cultivators of adventure sports, is that they throw themselves into danger because of situations that emerge in a particular moment of their lives and cause an imbalance in their psychic state.

Trauma, death drive

This imbalance is the conjunction of grief, anguish, and unmanageable representations in subjects unable to tolerate and metabolize them; it exceeds their Ego's capacity for response and installs them in a traumatic situation (Baranger and Mom, 1987).,

I will dwell on some of the consequences derived from this trauma.

One of them is a dynamic imbalance of drives, whose effects are the unbinding and release of some amounts of death drive. It may be experienced as a sensation of disrupting anguish, of annihilation, similar at times to panic. It seriously affects various integrative psychic functions and the ability to think and to symbolize.

The greater the traumatic effect, the closer the individual is to nameless terror, dread, or pure trauma in its economic modelling (Baranger and Mom, 987).

Once the discharge is facilitated by the action, the subject throws himself into danger, as if to deceive the Superego, when in fact, he or she submits masochistically to it.

Under these conditions, it is impossible to carry out any mourning work, and in this, I agree with Green (1986) when he says that "... the Tanathotic search would be one of the radical ways to oppose mourning work and hinder the processes of transformation and objectification ..." This kind of mourning is felt as insurmountable by Matías and unbearable by Tomás.

At the root is the masochistic coexistence of pleasure/pain that gives rise to it, which in these cases we equate with pleasure/risk; for these individuals, there is neither pleasure nor displeasure but something that could only be defined in terms of tensional intensity.

Likewise, there are differences between these two patients in that Matías finds himself in a more radical situation; he is more installed in a deceptive addiction close to perverse masochism. In him, there is a need to extricate the phantasm of the fulfilment of the parental desires of death (abortion) so as to be, paradoxically, someone whose death is desired beyond anything else. Matías fantasizes about imagining how many people would gather on the day of his wake, putting together pieces of his story – which is precisely what he cannot do. It seems that only death could unite them.

Matías is a prisoner of traumatic states of extreme anguish, emptiness, unbearable mourning, as well as of deadly identifications. He describes himself by saying "I am an adrenaline addict, one of those you mention in the article"; this description gives him essence and identity and allows him *to be* beyond what he *does* or what he *has*, including his most split aspects. And it spurs him to search, to insistently ask the reasons why. He does it in a sporty way as if the analytical process were a different kind of adventure, including the explicit challenge of confronting what he finds most disturbing if I can deal with him if historization and disidentification are possible.

Tomás, on the other hand, represents the paradigmatic situation of those who throw themselves into adventure and (more limited) risks at vital moments in which the impacts they must absorb and the transformations they must make threaten their narcissistic organization affecting their sense of self (identity). This feeling suffers breaks (rekindling of past mournings, his children's departure, the divorce process) and changes. The impossibility of putting these changes into practice and their traumatic effect makes him fear to fall into an unmanageable mental disorganization, and this leads him to a discharge into two channels: the body and action. In order to sustain the mental balance and to continue recognizing himself in the midst of chaos, he seeks to lean on the body, and so his sensations and senses pass to the foreground. This allows this kind of individuals to feel and be felt: to be through feeling.

The body acts as a buffer (Bleger, 2012) that protects the psyche from disorganization when a certain tolerable level of reintrojections is exceeded and supports the weight of this process. On the other hand, the action and discharge that sport and adventure provide serve as a framework for revitalizing experiences. Tomás' phrase makes sense: "There I felt alive again". It explains his way of counteracting the death experiences and mourning that were to come.

Narcissism, identity

In the two cases described, as in many others related to adventurous and risky sports, some aspects linked to the changes of the subject's sense of identity and narcissistic organization are brought into play.

The feeling of identity refers to something felt, to an inner expectation supported by the construction of identity. It requires points of reference and milestones to sustain it. L. Grinberg (1990) proposes that there are three kinds of integration: spatial, temporal, and social. These links cross the body and sexual identity in different evolutionary moments (adolescence, adulthood, mature age), each with its respective crisis, vicissitudes of object relations, and processes of belonging to significant groups and institutions.

The changes, mourning, and anguish connected with them will generate shocks or swings in the feeling of oneself and will test the durability or change of the cohesion and harmony of the Ego. This includes processes such as migrations, emotional separations (divorce, death of parents, emancipation of children), changes in work, etc. In all these cases, there will be experiences of losses and the need of re-encounter with oneself or with those parts of oneself involved in all these bonds.

In the so-called narcissistic pathologies, the identity is frequently threatened and the limits of the self become diffuse and unstable. The interest of the individuals is mostly focused on themselves, on their image, and on how they are seen and accepted/rejected by others, which leads to very intense states of anger or disappointment, or of joy and exaltation, depending on their reaction. The value of their Ego, synonymous with their self-esteem, is a constant concern. It is very difficult for them to discriminate themselves from others and to recognize their differences (their otherness). They tolerate very badly the ups and downs of the bonds of dependence that cause them to suffer abandonment/alienation or excessive intrusion and often make them resort to defensive or compensatory mechanisms to preserve their threatened Ego.

The feeling of vital emptiness, so often confused with dissatisfaction or discontent, is quite frequent. At its base, we find the loss or lack of constitution of diverse Ego functions and the excessive suffering derived from it. In the treatment of narcissistic pathologies, tedium, boredom, and the sensation of emptiness are expressed in this way or by their defensive counterpart: the search of vivifying experiences through adventures, the new, the unknown, and the exciting. All of them cover up the sensations of failure, suffering, and inner emptiness. The greater the need for such stimuli, the greater will be the inner fear of Ego dissolution, of unbearable suffering.

Returning to our two cases, Matías needs to erogenize the danger to compensate for very severe erogenization deficits that have been present throughout his life history. There is no voluptuous libido in him but rather a narcissistic hypersensitivity. He suspects that the joyousness he feels in those situations is close to a mortal pleasure. This was the reason why he came to the analysis. He is subjected to the parental desire of not having been born and almost fails to establish any erogenous relationship with his present loving objects.

The underprivileged (deprived individuals, vagrants, prostitutes) whom he must help or "save" represent split parts of his Ego that were haunted and threatened by very traumatic experiences almost without mental represent-ability. Matías is persecuted by a terrifying ghost (castrator): that of being unwanted by any woman or by anyone at all. We ask ourselves: what is the risk that such a patient cannot ever take? Possibly love, the Oedipal confron-tation, where all his needs and deficiencies would be exposed in raw flesh. Jealousy is for him the hell so feared, but it is substituted (like in all perverse rituals) by the danger of erotized death, replacing the danger that any love relationship represents for his phallic narcissism. In the face of the failure of the object's erogeneity, the narcissistic libido becomes sadomasochism.

Matías can be loved, but can he be desired? He was neither much desired by his mother nor is now much desired by his wife. When the lashing tails of an intense anguish appear, they connect him to the mourning for the lost libido. It is the model or pattern of actual neurosis.

Unlike obsessive neurotics, who do not want to risk anything, who pre-vent everything, who ruminate but do not act, Matías throws himself into the abyss of the vertigo ... Whom is he thus challenging? Possibly a father who, like Schreber's, represents an omnipotent figure whose actions know no limit. A father whom he tries to overcome by being more than him to others: the magnanimous, the almighty, the one who runs unspeakable dangers of all kinds, even at the risk of dying and finding there the fault, the longed-for limit that may brutally mark him forever. In this scenario, the adrenaline that stim-ulates and excites him would act as a signifier of the phallic (the fault is placed in the other), as a stopper to the consciously sought danger. He installs him-self in an omnipotent and triumphant place over the fault that he is evading. All this scaffolding and defensive armour functions as both a self-calming and self-exciting mechanism of his Ego and periodically protects him from the lack, from the fact of not being desired.

It can be said that Matías' emotional lability is more structural in kind and that of Tomás is an effect of the circumstances.

Bibliography

Baranger, M., W. and Mom, J. (1987), 'El trauma psíquico infantil, de nosotros a Freud, trauma puro, retroactividad y reconstrucción', *Rev Psicoanálisis*, T 4, Buenos Aires, Asociación Psicoanalítica Argentina.

Bichi, E. (2003) *La fase de "anidamiento" – Proceso o no proceso en el trabajo psicoanalítico Revista de Psicoanálisis*, Tomo IX, N° 4, Bs As. Buenos Aires: Asociación Psicoanalítica Argentina.

Bion, W. (1963) *Elements of psychoanalysis*. London: Routledge.

Bleger, J. (2012) *Symbiosis and ambiguity.* London: Routledge.

Botella César y, S.B. (2004) *The work of psychic figurability: Mental states without representation.* London: Routledge.

Deutsch, H. (1926) 'A contribution to the psychology of sport', *International Journal of Psychoanalysis*, 7, 223–227.

Freud, S. (1905) *Three essays on the theorie of sexuality*, standard ed., vol VII.

Freud, S. (1911) *Formulations on the two principles of the mental functioning*, standard ed., vol XII.

Freud, S. (1915) *Drives and their vicissitudes*, standard ed., vol XIV.

Freud, S. (1920) *Beyond the pleasure principle*, standard ed., vol XVIII.

Freud, S. (1924) *The economic problema of masochism*, stándard ed., vol XIX.

Green, A. (1999) *The work of the negative.* London: Free Association Books.

Green, A. (1986) *Life narcissism, death narcissism.* London: Free Association Books.

Hornstein, L. (2003) *Intersubjetividad y clínica.* Paidós.

Grinberg, L.Y.R. (1990) *The goals of psychoanalysis, identification, identity and supervision.* London: Karnac Books.

Marty, P. (1992) *Psicosomática del adulto.* Amorrortu Ed.

Winnicott, D. (1971) *Playing and reality.* London: Routledge.

Chapter 3

Fanaticism

This mental state and its derived behaviours both in individuals and in masses or groups are a source of concern and study nowadays, particularly because of the consequences in the form of violence and destruction that they bring to growing sectors of the population.

However, this is not a new problem: from early civilizations, we find its traces in violent expressions of religiosity. The rites and sacrifices propitiated by the goddess Cybele (originally from Phrygia, Asia Minor, and later from Rome), with priests who went so far as to self-mutilate, are one of its earliest examples. From there comes the original meaning of the verb: *fanor, fanaticus*.

"Fanatic" derives from the Latin *fanum*, which refers to the treeless space in which the sky can be seen. It is there that the light and also the sacred are manifested. Derivatively, *fanum* means a temple, a consecrated place.

More recently, the groups of fanatics that political ideologies and sport bring together are no less virulent than their religious predecessors.

Attempts have been made to approach and understand this phenomenon from various disciplines. Sociology has approached the problem focusing on the origin and vicissitudes of fundamentalism. Fundamentalism is generally defined from a religious perspective; the term has its origin in the North American Protestants of the 19th century, who advocated adherence to a set of principles and values of intransigent and strict application, among them the reading and literal interpretation of biblical or sacred texts, the reverent respect for ceremonies, tradition as something valuable and immovable. Thomas Meyer characterized it as a movement of arbitrary exclusion, a tendency opposed to the process of general openness of thought and the taking of initiatives, an enemy of the particular social forms of life that characterize modernity.

It would be a reaction "against" something, based on the perception of an enemy that threatens or promotes cultural and social changes as a result of secularization and modernity. This reaction is embedded in a moral and evaluative critique, where it is argued that things are not working well at the social and community level, and a return to a religious past and an idealized social order governed by hierarchy and patriarchy is postulated.

DOI: 10.4324/9781003293569-4

Faced with this, fundamentalism condemns any possible alternative and seeks to offer in exchange absolute certainties, firm support, intolerance of dissent, permanent help, unquestionable orientation, and refuge behind the closed security of absolute foundations. This closed position revolves around a fantasy of purity and integration as well as of communitarian sense and continuity (A. Giddens). He adds that "fundamentalism is not the same as fanaticism or authoritarianism. Fundamentalists call for a return to the scriptures and basic texts, which should be read literally, and propose that the doctrines derived from such readings be applied to social, economic or political life. Fundamentalism gives new vitality and relevance to the guardians of tradition".

From the religious perspective, be it that of the Gospels, the Torah, or the Koran, all of them offer a truth emanating from divine sources to which every human being should adhere, lest they walked their lives on the path of evil and perdition. Gathering behind its slogans is a way of protecting oneself from the loss of identity or identity referents (M. Castells). The only righteous life is one in which conduct derives from the law of God, as transmitted by those who act as "intermediaries" between God and mankind. From this conviction stems the aggressive vocation of the fundamentalist, as well as his proclivity to fanaticism and dogmatism: the truth that one possesses must not only be protected from all external "contamination" but also be propagated by whatever means necessary.

For other authors, fundamentalisms should be treated as social movements. Samuel Huntington, for example, argues that fundamentalism provides answers on how to deal with the chaos caused by secularism, scientific culture, and economic development, which would lead to the "clash of civilizations".

Over time, the concept of fundamentalism was extended to the economic, political, social, and cultural fields. Joseph Stiglitz alluded to neoliberal and market fundamentalism by referring to the economic policy of the IMF. F. Hinkelammert, in turn, states that the (social and economic) system becomes blind, denies the subject, and therefore cultures – threatened by the homogenization process generated by the world market – make fundamentalisms emerge to reconstitute reality and the realism of life.

In literature, the writer Amos Oz states, in his book *How to cure a fanatic*, that "the essence of fanaticism lies in the desire to force others to change. It is the tendency to improve the neighbor, mend the wife, make the child into an engineer or straighten the brother, instead of letting them be. Fanatics are most generous creatures. They are great altruists, often more interested in others than in themselves. They want to save your soul, to redeem you. Free you from sin, from error, from smoking. Free you from your faith or lack of faith. Fanatics are more interested in the other than in themselves for the simple reason that they have a rather meager self or no self at all".

In fact, those who with terrorist acts want to destroy other cultures or civilizations seek to save our souls and free us from our fateful and corrupt values, so that we may make our own the true, pure ones.

Oz cautiously suggests that there might be antidotes that could immunize us partially and in a limited way against fanaticism, imagination being one of them. He believes that if a person is able to imagine what his or her ideas imply, that already entails a slight improvement. Literature could also be an antidote by injecting imagination. "Read literature and you will be cured of your fanaticism. Unfortunately, many poems, stories and plays have been used throughout history to instill hatred and nationalistic moral superiority instead". He quotes Israeli poet Yehuda Amichai, who said, "Where our reason prevails, no flowers grow".

The other medicine Oz recommends against this scourge is a sense of humour. It is, according to him, a great remedy, and he finishes off his work by saying that he has never in his life seen a fanatic with a sense of humour.

In this work, I shall attempt to delve into the psychoanalytic roots underpinning the mental functioning of the fanatic. To this end, I will discuss the way in which beliefs are expressed, the involvement of passion, the identification and existential problems, and group expressions of fanaticism.

Love, passion

The passionate experience drags the subject, as an unexpected event imposed on him or her, transporting him or her from the consensual reality to a state where reason is swept away, any criticism disappears and the will dies. It is like a state of alienation, of self-estrangement. The subjects are not seduced by the object of their passion but are as if enchanted, almost hallucinated, totally given over to that unique and exclusive object that guides their behaviour and with respect to which they feel an urgent, imperative need. Nothing and no one can replace such an object, without which they feel they are at risk of annihilation.

The structural split of the Ego becomes evident in these situations. The fanatic longs for a situation of oceanic fusion with that object, for the re-edition of a pre-Oedipal, dyadic experience, which seeks to make the subject/object limits disappear through a joyful union with that whole. His/her Ego is almost completely captured, as if paying a price for the gift of absolute certainty.

This is something that cannot be repressed or suppressed. It is a remnant of the later, Oedipal, structural repression of the Ego, revived by a need that is savagely imposed on it. As J. Chasseguet says, there would be a return to the primary fusion between the Ego and the Ego Ideal in order to avoid anguish, castration, and conflict. An attempt is made to keep the subject in the range of illusion, longing for the oceanic feeling and making everything that hinders the fulfilment of that illusion disappear. The vital experience is, so to speak, emptied of authentic content.

Fanatics' link with the object of their passion is characterized by suffering, asymmetry, and the need for an identifying support. The fanatics will seek in that object calm and relief from their hardships, but this is always fleeting and transitory. Nor will they ever achieve a peaceful harmony, but rather a stormy equilibrium. They will be always suffering. This suffering state is correlated with the need for the object, which takes on an alienating character, for it will demand the immolation of their own thought as the price to be paid in order to preserve the reassuring certainty, the absence of doubt.

The object is a source of pleasure and suffering at the same time, but the subject cannot do without it. He or she needs it as a vital support, because without it, he or she would fall into the Thanatotic void and remain without representation of support, without any cathexis: would become a nothingness.

The object will never fulfil the subject's desires, never give rise to the fullness he or she expects; however, if the latter dare to decathect it, to walk away frustrated and suffering, the threat of decathexis brings him or her back again and again to that alienating swing. One seduces with his/her sole being, and the other is confused and frightened of becoming a nothingness. The emotional surrender to a kind of action and guided by an overvalued idea of the object of passion comes very close to a delusional system.

We can ask ourselves how the adhesion to these bonds is generated. The truth is that the greater the lack of primitive drive satisfaction, and the more generous the offer of a non-empathic object, the greater the unbound nostalgia and anguish. The subject is exposed to the lack of an object that helps, organizes, and cathects him or her, and to the presence of an object that traumatizes and alienates. This leads to opening oneself to a passionate experience, seeking to stanch the wound caused by the lack of authentic contents that permeates the life experience of the fanatics. They attached the passion to an exalted content, either of love or hate, with the sudden irruption and the urge of an uncontrollable discharge.

The passionate relationship is asymmetrical. The Ego maintains with its object a bond of necessity such that the object becomes the exclusive source of its pleasure. Being the interaction thus configured, the Ego considers itself as the only pole of suffering, and supposes that its object is exempt from it, far from the reach of suffering. It imagines that the object is enjoying an extreme pleasure to which it would not have access, from which it would be excluded. It is as if it must suffer in order to be able to love. In this clear bond, there is a predominance of Thanatos and the latent possibility of throwing the Ego into physical and psychical death. Only in the intervals in which there is a truce with Eros can pleasure manifest itself.

The need and dependence on the object have the characteristic of leading the Ego to experience suffering according to its greater or lesser need for a pleasurable object. The greater the need, the greater the suffering of the Ego, since the object withholds its presence or refuses to share the demanded cathexis. A source of pleasure and an effect of suffering at the same time, the object places the Ego in a paradoxical dilemma: if it wants to escape from suffering, it runs the risk of losing the pleasurable object; if it decides to preserve it, it exposes itself to a great suffering in exchange for a few crumbs of pleasure.

The emerging dynamic dramatically evidences how an object is erotically cathected. It is a vital identifying support for the Ego that at the same time puts it in danger of being thrown into the Thanatic void, of remaining without representation or investiture, of becoming nothing. This is so insofar as the object does not fulfil the promised satisfaction entirely (it never does) or does not allow the hope of fulfilment expected from it. It forcefully leads the subject to have to decathect it, to move away from that object that makes him or her suffer. Depending on the subject's degree of tolerance to suffering, the danger of decathexis and, consequently, the risk of Thanatic predominance will be greater or lesser.

But, in addition, there is another pressing issue: passion has no waiting time. It is now or never.

Alienation, a variant of passion, presupposes the cancellation of one's own thought, dazzled by the longed-for promise of the absence of suffering and conflict, guaranteed from the alienating object to the Ego as a gift. The price to pay is very high: it implies the immolation of one's own thought. Like Faust's, who sold his soul to the devil in order to preserve his absolute certainty, the audacity to question the thought of the other, to enter into conflict with that other's thought without fearing the elimination of one of the two thoughts. All this is a necessary condition for the development and evolution of psychic activity.

The uniqueness takes the place of the diverse and the different; unilaterality is the barren territory of fundamentalisms and fanaticisms, whether political, religious, social, sporting, etc. Oz (2011) says: "The fanatic is, in fact, someone who only knows how to count up to one".

It is helpful to compare fanatics with passionate lovers, who long for the encounter and fusion with their object, which they have idealized. There is between them a symmetrical bond of reciprocity, a balance of suffering and pleasure where doubt, insecurity, conflict, and even aggression are possible, but not hate. If there is a certainty, it is shared and oriented towards mutual pleasure.

The love relationship entails a task of mutual construction, of creativity shared by both lovers. This complementarity can lead to abandoning the vicious circle of narcissism, that of "to love so as not to get sick", in order to start the virtuous circle epitomized in the popular Brazilian saying: *Amor, energía que nao se esgota, quanto mais amor se gasta, mais bonito o amor brota* (Love, energy that doesn't run out, the more love is spent, the more beautiful it sprouts).

The fanatics have a pact with Thanatos, which in the name of a faith, of purity, of a political party, of the supreme ideals or values of society, leads them – as has happened so many times throughout history – to try to annihilate, destroy or degrade verbally or physically their opponent or infidel of the moment (their loving faith, their soccer team, their nation, their ideology).

Beliefs

To believe is to take for certain a thing that is not proven or demonstrated. However, this idea is considered true and certain and implies the tendency to act in relation to what is believed as if it really existed. Beliefs are most evidently manifested when divergences arise with respect to what is perceived as real. They are, therefore, a modification of the reality principle to resolve conflicting situations and to express the believer's desires (e.g., belief in another life modifies the meaning of the perception of death). It organizes the perception of reality by making the subject declare as existent something in which he or she can believe. Things are seen or considered according to what the individual believes them to be, and this determines both his/her ideas and his/her emotional or affective reaction.

Beliefs are established and influence the psychic organization by family or social influences, or by circumstances that the subjects have to go through in their time. From a social perspective, they fulfil an integrating function, since sharing a set of beliefs provides bonds of identity and belonging.

Although the fact of believing is an indispensable function in the structuring of the psyche and in the organization of the mind, beliefs are, in particular, representational contents that can be substituted or modified.

Etymologically speaking, "to believe" means "to have confidence".

Freud used the concept of belief in 1911, including it as a part of thinking equivalent to judging the external world, a mechanism he attributed to the Ego. In *The Future of an Illusion* (1927), he speaks of religious beliefs as a treasure trove of representations whose psychic origin is the desire to overcome the helplessness and vulnerability of the human being by creating the idea of an all-powerful father or higher intelligence that will guide humanity towards the good. Religion brings enormous relief to the psyche as it offers a universally accepted solution. In this system, religious beliefs show how the Ego can satisfy its desires through thinking without falling into delirium or creating a work of art.

Interested in the relationship of subjects with their beliefs, Freud describes this relationship as a deformed appreciation of material reality put at the service of defending psychic reality. From the moment subjects think, they also believe and, probably, believe what they desire. The use of belief has similarities with that of the distorted representation subsequent to suppressing a representation. Belief acts as a protective mechanism to strengthen the suppression of that which is not recognized as such. It not only withdraws a representation considered doubtful; more radically, it takes it to a state or place where there is no contradiction or doubt whatsoever. In this sense, Freud argues that beliefs should be considered as a form of punishment. Thus understood, a belief would be equivalent to annulling the realization of a desire perceived as dangerous.

He considers religious representations as illusions, taking by illusion "a belief when its motivation is, above all, to strive for the fulfillment of desire; and in this we dispense with its nexus with effective reality, just as the illusion itself renounces its testimonies". From this perspective, an illusion is not the same as an error, nor is it necessarily an error. What characterizes belief is that it always derives from human desires. Taking this to the religious realm, belief is based on a wish fulfilment about the afterlife.

How does the subject adhere to beliefs? Basically, this happens when unconscious fantasies loaded with a strong desiderative quantum succeed in making the Ego, with its function of belief, give them the status of reality. In this way, they acquire power over mental functioning. Thus belief is taken for true even if it is not, unlike knowledge, which is that which has been proved to be true.

Belief, then, is based on probability, not on certainty, but has as its correlate an emotional state of confidence that accompanies the state of certainty. The fanatics do not hesitate. They have an obstinate and almost delirious certainty, whatever the circumstances.

Their adherence to an overvalued idea or emblem places them in a place where their own thought (and very often that of others) is annulled, and they will boast, their ideas insufflated with omnipotence, that castration does not make a dent in them. Their object/emblem does not admit to any discussion or questioning. It has an idealized character, endowed with the most precious qualities and virtues.

Beliefs are based on the only possible interpretation of reality, and the content of their hyperconcrete statements is engraved in an indisputable way, leading to states of devotion. This mortar, born in turn from distressing experiences of emptiness, welds the fanatics to their ideas. Moreover, they use the willingness to believe, but coagulating its meaning and being at the same time deceived by it.

In "That Incredible Need to Believe", Julia Kristeva (2006) states that the concepts developed by Freud in describing oceanic feeling and primary identification include two key moments in which believing takes root. She defines oceanic feeling as "a jubilant osmosis of the subject into the common flesh of the 'not-yet-self' swallowed by a 'not-yet-world'". It is the intimate union of the self and the surrounding world experienced as an absolute certainty of satisfaction and security, but at the same time as a loss as far as the self is concerned. It is a prelinguistic experience dominated by sensations, and it leads to a sensory and mental plenitude, a feeling of indubitable certainty that would be at the root of believing.

Regarding primary identification, Freud posits a pre-Oedipal identification with the father of personal prehistory, a loving father with the attributes of both father and mother, as he explains in *The Ego and the It*. A father who is a symbolic stranger and who will replace the horror and fascination of the oceanic feeling by offering the child love and a symbolic and linguistic order. He is the one who loves the mother and is loved by her, with a love that leaves room for the child's self and offers him love as a subject. The words of the father, source of authority and law, will be the words of the child and will transform the anguish into a believing expectation. "I believe, thus I speak". It is the father's listening that gives meaning to the child's speech. In this listening, the child gradually generates his autonomy with respect to the mother while at the same time constituting himself as a speaking and desiring subject before the father. The speaking being is a believing being. Primary identification, the basis of authority, is constituted by the love that acknowledges the symbolic being of the baby, conferring on it its dignity of being. The reject of the need to believe leads to the fall of authority. The believing self can express what it feels metaphorically and not lose itself completely. Primary identification causes it to find its reverse in the need to know, to ask questions.

The fanatics do not have access to all this. For them, there is no question to be asked. In the chapter "About reality. Knowing or certainty" of her book *The Lost Sense*, Piera Aulagnier proposes that "knowing demands that we renounce the certainty of what is known. Wanting certainty implies refusing to recognize that all knowledge is coextensive with a continuous movement". That is, it is a flow, something neither static nor perennial. Dario Sor (2010) states that "fanaticism is born in the mysterious babbling of the grammar of reverie, which gives shape to the first intelligible words of emotional language". This would require the recipient to be in a peculiar situation, which he calls "devotion". In order to inject devotion into the other, into his ideas, it is necessary to have a special ability.

At its origin, the non-thinking of the fanatic is based on the failure to create and organize a fabric of networks of tolerance that may sustain and make possible the growth and transformation of a mind in a state of evolution. According to Bion's conceptualization, there would be a failure in the maternal reverie function that prevents the infant from developing a rudimentary consciousness, necessary to acquire psychic quality. We speculate that such consciousness must spiral upward in order to cross the sensory gap and thus gain access to the experience of human contact with the mother.

Sor says that the fanatic idea is the "maximal idea": a mono-idea or dog-matic idea without articulation with other ideas. Ideational isolation takes place as a process in which obstinacy has a big role. Initially, it calms anxiety and makes uncertainty disappear, so that the pain and discomfort they produce can be avoided. In the ideational exchange, when other ideas approach, it is as if they stick to it, as if the free or independent idea were oversaturated.

For this kind of ideas, plurality, exchange, coexistence, transformation, the possibility of a crisis are unacceptable. It is absolute and repels any hint of doubt.

Any object can be used as a maximal idea. We differentiate it from the psychotic ideation, the delusional idea which does not achieve a realization, a confirmation in reality. Delusions and hallucinations would be the stuff that fills this gap.

For this author, there are three types of thoughts:

a   Those apt to be thought, which possess a causal structure and are at the service of the formulation of ludic, scientific, and aesthetic thinking. They make it possible to create, transform, conserve and evolve what is thought.
b   Those that enter into transformation in hallucinosis.
c   The fanatical non-thoughts, which dispense with reason. There is an absence of conflict in them. Sor defines them as a complex form of a maximal idea.

The fanatics' devotion is equal to the non-existence of thought, of knowledge. They superimpose contents that are not thought, while the latter is deprived of its symbolic and modelistic value. Fanaticism stupidizes, its statements are hyperconcrete ("blacks have a bad smell", for example). It uses pseudo-models and parables instead of metaphors and analogies.

The parable has only one possible interpretation and serves to engrave in fire a restricted and indisputable concept.

As Sor (2010) says, the devotion of the fanatics is equal to the inexistence in them of thinking, of knowledge. Their faith leads them to have a single, superior and dogmatic idea, to which they cling by reaffirming their preeminence over others, in a clear asymmetry.

Their regressive mentality leads them, on the one hand, to simplify: there are good people and bad people, and "those like me are the good ones". On the other hand, instead of obedience to an authority, it generates authoritarianism (according to the model of the Ideal Ego). In the name of noble and lofty goals, it demands blind, uncritical submission.

In terms of development, Canzler compares groups and subjects in their process of separation-individuation, following Winicottian approaches on transitional spaces, which allow to tolerate independence, separation, narcissistic wound, and pain due to loss of omnipotence. Although fanatics are also motivated by their objects and ideas, and the groups of fanatics zealously defend their ideologies and idols, there are important differences.

1   The reality principle is attenuated.
2   Knowledge and acknowledgement of individual responsibility have disappeared.
3   The end is negated and its psychic consequences are altered.
4   Object losses, destructiveness, and catastrophes are also negated.
5   Tolerance of ambivalence is replaced by splitting off.
6   Abandonment of triangulation for fused states.

As mentioned above, this kind of thought is handled with hyperconcrete statements, with little symbolic or modelistic value, and with a predominance of parables instead of analogies and metaphors.

Need of identification: a clinical vignette

Let's look at the situation of Deborah, 15 years old, who comes to the clinic brought by her parents. The previous weekend she had ingested 20 pills of a tranquillizer (Clonazepam 0.5 mg) from a bottle her mother had, with the intention of ending up forever with her intolerable suffering.

After having undergone a gastric lavage in an emergency room and being hospitalized for two days, she was advised to begin a psychological treatment.

Since our first interview, this slim, languid, and childlike-faced teenager shattered scraps of her life in a torrent of words, as if a pressure valve would have been suddenly opened. She attends one of the most prestigious schools in Buenos Aires and is a brilliant student. Her parents, both successful professionals ("people of high intellectual flight", as she describes them), have always been absorbed by their work, meetings, commitments, and have proposed to her, their only daughter, to stand out, to grow permanently, to be remarkable, as a goal for her life.

They have devoted very little time to attend to her most basic and primary emotional demands. Their professional occupations were always a priority. Debora puts a great deal of emotional distance in telling the story, in a tone of bitter reproach.

Shortly after entering secondary school, she began to take an interest in politics and almost immediately became a fervent member of a political party. There he met Germán (17 years old), with whom she had been having an ardent and intense love affair for a year. "The first and only one in my life", she says.

Two months ago, in a "crisis of conscience", Germán broke off with the party, from which he decided to radically move away. Since he made this decision, there were almost daily arguments, brawls, and fights with Debora, who held firmly to her political ideals and militancy.

Values, ideology, betrayal, etc., are the issues that distance them now, until last week, when Germán decided to put an end to the relationship.

"I fell into a total, absolute vacuum", said Deborah. "My life ceased to have any meaning. I suddenly lost everything that had been supporting me. I can't go back to the party either, nothing can be the same as before".

Only a few hours pass between these experiences, narrated as an unbearable pain, and her decision to put an end to her life. Desperately, she resorts to the first thing she finds at hand, that bottle of pills.

Deborah now clings to her analytical process like a lifesaver, attending sessions almost daily and striving to be "a good patient". In this context, she has started to ask herself about the hows and whys of her life, her ways of bonding, her emotional demands, and her ideals. This transition is marked by an idealized transference, which then turns to eroticism and finally leads to her project of studying medicine after the secondary school. Her expectation of becoming a posteriori a "psychoanalytic fanatic" is a very high risk and will demand an intense analytical work in the future.

In Deborah, as in other subjects with a structure of fanaticism, the desire for oceanic fusion together with the search for an emblematic father figure is quite evident. This father will have to offer absolute certainty and truth and be an idealized and all-powerful figure, not castrated. To the religious fanatic, this place is occupied by the figure of God.

These individuals need figures/representatives whose statements produce a kind of hypnotic submission, whose ideas/orders have a unique way of being interpreted, are immutable and unquestionable, and first and foremost, whose superiority over all opponents is clearly shown.

In "Psychology of the Masses" (1921), Freud argues that the concept of the Ego Ideal explains particularly well the fascination of love, the dependence on the hypnotist, and the submission to the leader; in all these cases, an outsider is placed by the subject in the place of his Ego Ideal.

Unlike the common neurotic – whose Ideal Ego is interior to the subject, depends on paternal values, is marked by castration and by the Superego, and refers to ethical values – the religious or political fanatics depend permanently on an exterior figure, seek omnipotent and infallible figures, propose altruistic ends (for the good of ..., justice for all, equality, etc.), but as regards themselves, they feel that they are as worthless as the rest. Perhaps this also explains why they kill or give their life (which has no value) for a cause.

Deborah reaches adolescence compensating for her deficiencies and primary affective voids with her intellectual brilliance, but the crises and the bereavements she has to face as an adolescent lead her to adopt the banners of her political party, a group that receives and contains her as a "prodigal daughter". Her amorous experience with Germán gave her the completeness she was longing for. At that time, she seemed more adult and precocious than many of her companions.

Later, the break-up leaves her Ego totally unarmed and helpless, making her to fall into a Tanathotic void that uncovers the ideological and amorous veils covering the lack.

These challenges have now reached the psychoanalytical process, which at the time has lasted for three years.

Existential problems, group issues

The fanatical subjects live (as exemplified) in a state of extreme narcissistic vulnerability. Their self, its cohesion and integrity, are felt as if they were suffering a permanent threat of dissolution.

The emblem or ideal in which they have found refuge becomes their necessary point of anchorage and support. They have the illusion of becoming, through the fusion, one and the same thing with the object, of being something at last. They dramatically perceive their inner emptiness; this disturbs their self-esteem, to the extent that it reaches the lowest points of the scale.

On the other hand, aware of their weakness, they seek refuge in groups or institutions that may shelter and protect them and to which they "give all their life and heart". Identifying, belonging and participating with the group also makes it possible for them to loosen the bonds of repression and find a momentary relief from orphanhood and misery.

While, on the one hand, the fanatic individual finds refuge and shelter in his extremist ideals, on the other hand, the fanatic position provides him with a mode of social bonding: total and absolute membership and blind militancy. All this conceals submission as an unconscious punishment together with the unconscious satisfaction of feeling "I am nothing", as opposed to that grandiose figure that is beyond castration and death, whose double would take on figurability in the fantasy of the world's salvation.

It is important to point out that in fanaticism, there is a leap from the individual to the social. The fanatical individuals may suffer in their intimacy, may even doubt, until they suddenly burst into the group, into society, into history, whereby their doubts dissipate and their fanatical attitude is intensified.

The pathology of narcissism allows us to understand the need to exalt above all the group or national emblem, exalting at the same time the participants's own Ego, together with their hostile contempt for others. From this perspective, anything that threatens the perfection of their emblem, party, team, or nation is felt as a threat to one's Ego, since the boundaries of the Ego are confused and have been expanded to become part of the mass of followers.

The need to maintain the cohesion and integrity of the group (or of the Ego) in the face of threats stimulates hatred, which functions as a sort of cement that binds, fixes, and solidifies. The narcissistic organization soon tends to acquire paranoid characteristics, making violence almost inevitable.

In this way, the group (and the Ego) becomes cohesive, united by hatred and by the existence of an enemy one has to hate and fight. Presumably, the more fragile the sense of one's own identity, the greater the need to amalgamate it by hating an enemy.

In an unconscious way, the fact of clinging to an illusory, idealized, or denigrated object/emblem/representation serves to avoid the experience of fragmentation or Ego disintegration, as well as to concentrate on that object the amounts of libido that sustain it. As for themselves, fanatics think they are nothing. The fanaticized belief, as a substitute for destructuring, gives certainty and a feeling of vitality, but not a genuine love for oneself or for another object.

From another conceptual viewpoint, expelling negativity, the rejected, the repressed, in short projecting the bad outwards to reinforce the feeling of inner goodness is an early psychical mechanism that may be assimilated at the group level to René Kaes' (1993) concept of "denial pact". He called thus "the set of unconscious agreements that, in every bond (of a couple, group, family or institution), condemns to the destiny of repression, denial or disavowal everything capable of questioning the formation and preservation of that bond and the burdens to which it is subjected, maintaining it under the form of the unrepresented and the imperceptible".

This mechanism has a double aspect that must be taken into account, since it simultaneously satisfies the psychic economy of the singular subject and that of the whole group. It has two polarities: one of them organizes the bond, and the other is defensive.

In a later stage, when the mass of fanatics' intolerance is accentuated within the paranoid ideation, cruel behaviour and insensitivity towards others (be them rivals or just different people) are exacerbated.

When the individuals' guilt feeling is dissolved in the mass, violent actions find a foothold by projecting into the opponent their inner emptiness, their lack of humanization. In this way, by removing the humanity traits from the other subjects, the exercise of evil is inevitably reached.

Any destructive action is fully justified and approved by the mass as a whole, whose members rationalize their hatred as being for the sake of the supreme ideal they feel to embody and defend. They see it as a beneficial, protective, purifying destruction.

Green argues that, in these cases, rather than jouissance, what predominates is the lack of sensitivity to what the attacked object/subject may experience. The aggression falls on the libidinal decathexis of the object. He calls "deobjectalization" the mechanism by which the individuals conceive their destroyed or attacked object as a thing. It could be said that this "dead passion", which dwells at the very centre of fanatics, has taken the place that would have corresponded to mourning if the conditions had been different.

How does fanaticism develop?

Martin Solar (2019) states that "it can be dwelled dormant slowly 'cooking' its ingredients in the fire of the home, a fire that feeds and guarantees almost for sure all the intellectual, behavioral and affective machinery that fanatic personalities have". He quotes Amos Oz (2011): "... very often it all starts in the family. Fanaticism begins at home, precisely because of the all-too-common urge to want to change a loved one for his or her own good [...]. It begins with the urge to tell a child: you have to be like me, not like your mother; or you have to be like me, not like your father; it does not tell him or her: please, be very different from both of us."

The mental functioning of the fanatic masks very severe deficits in the constitution of the self, and in the peculiarities of the primary object-*infans* exchange from its earliest stages.

The inability to tolerate any absence, the unconscious experience of the child as an extension of oneself, as someone neither separated nor differentiated from the mother, all this configures a state of hyperpresence and strongly influences the infant's psyche. This split mode of functioning predisposes to the projection of intolerable feelings, especially hatred and anguish, that need to be expelled.

These structural failures of maternal narcissism gravitate on the child's psyche and potential identity. It is as if their own identity were annulled, kidnapped, at the expense of the narcissism of others, and exposed to the inoculation of thoughts and feelings that may become fanatical.

Martín Solar affirms that the lack of security and confidence in the founding narcissistic structuring gives rise to an "escalation", to arrogance and then to omnipotence ("I can handle anything"). We are in the territory of malignant narcissism. The child's identification with this intense maternal omnipotence is one of the very first foundations of future fanatical functioning.

The intrusion experiences are inscribed as traumatic traces that may be repeated in the future when different situations are activated. The unquestionable mandates that have penetrated the mind of the child that is potentially a future fanatic become adhesive, like a sticker.

The structuring of a trophic narcissism would allow the infant's own original capacities and articulations to develop, a process that is here interfered with. This incapacity generates the painful need to repeat in a concrete and exact way mandates and prohibitions to which the child is totally subjected, and therefore must renounce to his/her own, autonomous, free thoughts.

Solar postulates that identificatory interference would have different destinies depending on whether it adopts an active or passive modality. In the passive mode, it is likely to function in a masochistic way, directing against oneself the deadly fanatical feelings that have been received. This may give rise to self-mutilation and sacrificial behaviours, as well as to the establishment of sadomasochistic bonds.

In the active mode, identification with the aggressor plays an important role. The aggressor can become an active and fervent fanatic leader (political, religious, etc.) who can drag crowds and seduce the masses with flaming speeches of vindication. With the fatuous search and aspiration to the Ego ideal, the individual would defend from the omnipotent trap of primary narcissism.

In this process of identifying with the aggressor, the Ego of the infant would be caught in a sort of limbo between the omnipotence of primary narcissism and a faint incipient aspiration to the Ego ideal. This would act as a promise referred to the object and would lead to secondary narcissism, the true narcissism of the Ego (Freud, 1921).

The ideal

The issue of the ideal is central to the understanding of the fanatic structure. Fanatics are fixed to an ideal Ego, conceived as a narcissistic ideal of omnipotence. This entails a primary identification with the mother, invested with omnipotence. It is not only the union of the Ego with the It. The ideal Ego serves as a support for what Lagache has called "heroic identification" (the identification with exceptional and prestigious characters). The psychic apparatus of the infant is governed by an ideal Ego with a very high narcissistic charge, without full access to the ideal of the Ego that goes hand in hand with the Oedipal resolution. All this entails the risk that Chasseguet-Smirgel (1985) calls "the excess of the ideal". This excess is so intensely fixated and so obstinate that it makes impossible any attempt to attenuate it.

In terms of economic dynamics, this very early primary identification, wholly invested with omnipotence, causes an oversaturation of the omnipotence charge of the object. The latter imposes itself and vehemently inoculates in the helpless and forming Ego of the infant the grandiosity of its omnipotent ideal Ego and the tyranny of its Superego.

Fanatics do not reach an objectalization of the ideal, since this implies adhering to a unique and irreplaceable value – as happens with the object cathexis in the amorous situation. Their impulse or aspiration does not follow this path.

The idealization process requires a subjective object to be produced, a product of the reciprocal idealization of the mother and the child. This never occurs in the fanatic, since symbolization and creation are covered by the "full emptiness" of certainties, where there is no separation or distance.

When fanatics go into the social realm, their ideal of omnipotence leads them to transform themselves into idols, and to this heroic mission, they surrender "body and soul", since they also form an indissoluble part of that *corpus*. Their beliefs are firmly welded with the sense of existence of their own being. The one who will restore honour, the leader of the people's demands, the "saviour", maybe a hero but is at the same time the one who offers himself/herself in sacrifice. These heroes hand over a great part of their psychic energy to the ideal; they spend their existence in reaching their goal and thus lose their own vitality. Illusorily, they hide part of this "self-love" by adhering to the emblem or fanaticized representation. This representation conceals under a grandiose cloak its emptiness of being, its lack of genuine and proper vitality.

Britton (1995) argues that these kinds of idols are unshakable, among other things because "abandoning beliefs involves mourning". It can be said that in the fanatic personality, the work of the first mourning, the renunciation of the infantile omnipotence of primary narcissism, has not taken place. Thus, what is at stake is not a stopped mourning but, in a way, a non-existent mourning.

The intergenerational factor plays an important role in all these processes, inasmuch as the stories of lack of elaboration of the mourning of infantile omnipotence, of desolation and helplessness, as well as of humiliations, deprivations, damages, insults, and vindications, are inoculated and transmitted from one generation to the other.

To the extent that in the course of an analytical process, subjects are able to position themselves before their system of ideals in a less persecutory and coercive way, relieved of the archaic super-Ego pressure that acts as a guarantee of subjective cohesion, dynamic changes may take place that allow to put distance from certain beliefs considered as irreplaceable dogmas.

Rafael Paz (2019) argues thus and suggests that revealing the genesis of personal idols, together with the "coming to light" of their nuclei of secret beliefs, lead to a different order of cohesion, stripped of the peremptoriness and infantile desperation that welds the subject to dogmatic organizations or to absolute values. By talking in the analysis about these absolute truths, they are in fact placed as relative truths, liable to be challenged; hence, the subject is encouraged "to be abandoned" by the archaic, persecutory, and idealized objects that these beliefs conceal.

This necessary upheaval of subjectivity runs through everything that supports defensive processes and narcissistic articulations.

Fanaticism in sports

Although structurally, all fanatical subjects have similar psychopathological and group functioning characteristics, it is important to recognize some particularities and differences, such as those that we will discuss with reference to the sports field.

Sports have had a massive diffusion in contemporary societies for the last 50 years. Both their practice and the show they offer have progressively increased due to the formidable business they give rise to and the incessant and exhausting penetration and propaganda that the mass media provide.

As a millenary product of culture, sport is functional to the needs of relaxation and recreation that derive from its playful character. It acts as a psychological moratorium making it possible for us to temporarily forget, while the game lasts, both our inner conflicts and the miseries that life imposes on us.

It achieves this task through evasion, since we immerse ourselves for a while in a creation where the compliance with the rules of daily reality is exchanged for those of pleasure/displeasure coming from the game itself. On the other hand, it allows us to release in a controlled way the aggressiveness that culture limits in its genesis.

The renunciation to the free expression of sexual and aggressive drives has as its cost a certain amount of cultural unrest. Sport has the character of a compromise, since it makes it possible to liberate that which is ordinarily forbidden: the desire to kill and to give free rein to destructiveness.

This is as valid for the actors as it is for the spectators, who, through a mechanism of identification, participate in the experience and live it by discharging the energy of their drives. An important release of pleasure is also achieved in this way.

Participation becomes more lively when there are rivals/spectators who, with their opposition, help to generate warlike and confrontational climates.

Often sheltered in the mass phenomena, but others belonging to a sports motto or jersey, the fans find a channel for their passion gathered in "barras bravas" (like the English hooligans) with the most brazen violence, but sometimes as lonely adherents (fans), "sick", "crazy" or suffering and passionate followers of the sports campaign of a club, for which they "give their lives".

Under these clothes, which may have a ritualized façade, when they go on weekends to support their favourite team, fans shamelessly display a private erotic scene, which they make public under the protection of the masses. These expressions range from unconditional love ("It's a feeling I can't stop", "I follow you everywhere, I love you more and more") to the most uncontainable violence.

A mere spectator may become a fan according to the ups and downs of the show, of the mass action, or of his private life, since any of them can ignite the flame of his sentimental outburst.

The adhesion to the jersey of a soccer club, for example, is like a paternal surname that is carried as if it were an attempt of genealogical continuity transmitted from father to offspring. That is why one of the first things many fans do when a child is born is to register him/her as a member of the club they love, perhaps much earlier than caring for his/her religious or community membership. This adhesion will become part of the subject in an indissoluble way and supposedly for the whole life. It is a strong identifying mark that survives, even more when changes in the self and in the feeling of identity go through states of crisis or destructuring as a result of migrations, change of marital status, bereavement, etc.

To belong, to participate, gives the subject protection against a sort of helplessness, especially that of being an anonymous being, a nobody, someone without any kind of blazons or identity marks.

Thus, for a father, the club of his love becomes the custodian and the (parental and regressive) protector of a part of his identity, as happens with religious believers. However, this devotion, which is also charged with faith and mysticism, only gives an account of the erotic aspect, of the objective bond, and of the need for identification. The fanatics add another element, imbued with Thanatotic components, which brings them closer to the position of the militants and the fundamentalists.

As we have already said, they orient their passion by their need and dependence on the cathected object as the only provider of calm and relief. This is not, though, a peaceful calm but a stormy one. Their pact with Thanatos will lead them, in the name of their faith, of purity, of their political party, of supreme ideals, or the values of their society, to seek to annihilate, destroy or verbally or physically degrade the opponent or infidel (to their loving faith, their motto, their team) – as has happened so many times throughout history.

There are classical rivals or enemies, the necessary antipode (Independiente vs. Racing, Boca vs. River in Argentina; Liverpool vs. Manchester United, Barcelona vs. Real Madrid in Europe). There are events where national identity is at stake, as in matches involving the country's national team, or during world championships. Through identification, when "the national team" plays, everyone recreates the experience of to be participating in the match. We suffer and enjoy, and we go from euphoria to dismay at the same time as those who are playing on the field. If they become the best team in the world, a little piece of us becomes the best too, because we feel them as a part of each of us. Every shout of a goal brings us closer to experiencing it. The World Cup, for example, is today a social event that touches the fibre of the national being, summoning everyone, men and women. In addition, to identify oneself, to belong and be part of a whole allows to loosen the bonds of repression and find relief for a while from orphanhood and misery.

Fanatics, on the other hand, adjust their banners every weekend and lash out against "the hated object". Their passion is guided not so much by love but by dread – the hatred that would deny the certainties of their being. Fan chants often emphasize their unwavering loyalty to their team and aggressive inclinations towards opposing teams, even going so far as to say they should kill them.

The above conceptualization emphasizes the logic of drives, the satisfaction of desire, sexual and generational similarities and differences in relationships. It aims at understanding the internal world, with its system of representations and objects. It is governed by the principle of identity, the judgments of attribution and existence, and the mechanisms of projection and introjection.

The verbs that are mainly conjugated in this universe are to be and to have, but it is interesting and relevant to be able to access other ways of understanding these processes, and other logics. From a perspective that highlights the bonding aspects, the uncertainty and the power relations between subjects, it is inevitable to be affected by the encounter/disencounter with the other. The latter, as a radical outsider, imposes his/her presence and otherness. The mechanism that operates is the judgment of presence (the decision to make room for the presence of the other as an outsider), defined by doing among others who are our equals, but at the same time, are different to us.

In the case of fanatics, the feeling of belonging may be experienced, then, by their inclusion in the mass. The identity exacerbation unifies them. Members of the mass are together, but not linked. The mass does not recognize any difference between supporters, sympathizers, and fans. Their beliefs and assumptions sustain the illusion of commonality as something that is identical and indiscriminate.

Unlike the belonging derived from being part of a whole, sports fans or sympathizers reaffirm their subjective heterogeneity.

Another clinical vignette

Since he was a child, Alberto (35 years old) used to go to the soccer stadium with his father, who integrated him as a companion and mascot to "that passionate and supporting gang" that every week met more to suffer (because of the low performance of their team) than for belonging to a sporting lineage of which they felt proud. It was one of the few spaces in which Alberto shared moments of union and attachment with his father, who by then was falling into a spiral of alcoholism. He had violent verbal disputes with his wife, who often accused and disqualified him, and prolonged absences from the home, until he finally disappeared from Alberto's life when he was 11 years old. They would meet again several years later, when Alberto was already an adult. His mother, "always nervous, always dissatisfied, demanding and exacting", formed another family when Alberto was 13. Although he had a place alongside his two female sisters and afterwards his half-brothers, he never again felt that he had "a nest of his own". He stumbled into the fourth year of secondary school, but left it to start working in a number of activities, all of them transitory, until the present.

At the request of his partner, Felisa (32), who was in her sixth month of pregnancy, Alberto agreed to have a consultation "before making any more mistakes in my life".

In the last few months, he returned continuously to the soccer stadium, becoming more and more passionate and fanatical, to the point of becoming part of the most violent gang of followers (the "*barra brava*"). He took part in fights and assaults to supporters of other teams, sometimes in the stadium, sometimes in the streets around it. He was taken away twice by the police and was delayed for a short time in each case.

His wife has turned on an alarm signal in her mind; she does not understand what is wrong with him, why he has suddenly become like this when he used to be a peaceful person, an affectionate companion. "Has he gone mad?", she asks herself. "Why all this rage over his sports club?"

Alberto has had two or three psychological consultations so far. He lives in a state of tension and restlessness that he cannot explain; it is like a sense of uneasiness that he can only calm down when he is with the gang shouting, jumping, encouraging his team, and sometimes hitting and insulting the incidental rivals. It is obvious that his new situation as a potential father forces him to confront his most archaic experiences searching for reference points and emblems that allow him to confront a task that he feels is beyond him. His current "nest" revives his expectations but also the pain of the emptiness he suffered.

He then resorts to those old emblems that he shared with his father, reediting with the mass of adepts not only the erotic aspects but also the growing flows of hatred that he had to repress and bury, but that now have found the means and the channel to express themselves. The enemies are out there.

In sports, the ideal does not lie in altruistic aims towards humanity, like in politics or religion, but in the projection of success (the best club, the most fervent fans, etc.). Alberto's attempts to regain his wounded or lost narcissism are short-circuited by the growing demands imposed on him as a husband and father. His life crisis must be processed so that the repetition of history is not passed on to the next generation.

Games between men, with the consequent ideas of rivalry and competition, physical contact, homosexual fantasies, etc., have its identifying referent, as Piera Aulagnier puts it, in "he who will be able to become a father ... whom the mother's discourse, but also the effective discourse pronounced by the paternal voice, designate as such".

The father, the first representative of others, of the sociocultural discourse, is thus the essential architect of the child's identification project. The bearer of the paternal function is designated "by law" to transmit a function that passes from father to father. If the "jersey" of the soccer team is like the paternal surname, an identifying mark that is worn almost invariably for the rest of one's life, to wear it is for the child a way of making sure that the one who gave him the jersey is *his/her father* and not

another; and for that father, it is a way of trying to guarantee his genealogical continuity.

Advertising songs for soccer matches have frequently emphasized out-
bursts of extreme emotion, such as screaming and crying, and draw attention to the fact that these feelings cannot be stopped and the participants
cannot escape them. In many cases, these feelings started when members
were taken to matches as very young children by their fathers.

Identification is the psychic process by means of which a subject makes
his/her own another subject's aspect, property, or attribute and transforms
himself/herself totally or partially following the model of the other.

There is no other way of generation of the identificatory project than the
transmission of the ideal of "being a father" from father to child. It is the only
"guarantee" of transcendence, of the illusion of immortality, of the acceptance of castration, on condition that the child takes the baton, becoming the
bearer of the Olympic flame of paternity and its emblems, which he/she in
turn will transmit to his/her own children.

The child will proclaim "what he/she wants to be when he/she grows up".
He/she will choose among the representational stock of desirable objects
offered by his/her parents: in our time, the identification with a soccer
emblem can be one of such objects.

This identification will be imaginary insofar as it comes from the set of
references that subjects can link to the image of themselves that will accompany them throughout their life. This identificatory knowledge includes a
series of emblematic values that have been cathected in an imaginary way
but which at the same time belong to the sociocultural discourse. It is also
a symbolic identification, since it transcends the real incarnation of the person representing that family function or role. By moving from the singular to the universal, the father and child roles become independent of that
which embodies them.

Let's add that somebody's adhesion to his/her emblematic flag, to his/
her club of belonging, puts him/her in one of four possible positions: sym-
pathizer, fan, fanatic or indifferent. Categories of "fan" and "fanatic" are
very changing and dynamic, so that one and the same individual may be in
one or the other in different circumstances of his/her life. It can be likened,
respectively, to love and passion relationships – with alienation as a variant
of the latter.

Bibliography

Armengol Millans R. (1999) 'El fanatismo, una perversión del narcisismo', *Soc.,
Española de Psicoanálisis*, IV.
Aulagnier P. (1980) *Los destinos del placer*. Barcelona: Petrel.
Aulagnier P. (2003) *The violence of interpretation. From pictogram to statement*.
London: Routledge.

Aulagnier, P. (1980) *El sentido perdido*. Buenos Aires: Ed Trieb.

Britton R. (1995) 'Psychic reality and unconscious belief', *International Journal of Psychoanalysis*, 1995(1).

Canzler, P. and Haynal, A. (1999) Sources of fanaticism, Bulletin 53 of European Psychoanalytic Federation.

Castells, M. (1998) *La era de la Información, El poder de la identidad*. Madrid: Alianza Ed.

Chasseguet-Smirgel, J. (1985) *The Ego Ideal*. London: Free Association Books.

Del, Valle. E., Belmonte Lara, O., Kargieman, A. and Saludjian D. (1976) *La identificación en Freud*. Buenos Aires: Edit Kargieman.

Diccionario Ilustrado de la Lengua Española, 1980.

Freud, S. (1914) *On narcissism*, standard ed., vol XIV.

Freud, S. (1921) *Group psychology and analysis of the Ego*, standard ed., vol XVIII.

Freud, S. (1927) *The future of an illusion*, standard ed., vol XXI.

Freud, S. (1930) *Civilization and its discontents*, standard ed., vol XXI.

Giddens, A. (2002) *Runaway world, how globalization is reshaping our lives*, London: Routledge.

Green, A. (1986) *Life narcissism, death narcissism*. London: Free Association Books.

Green, A. (1990) *On private madness*. London: Karnac Books.

Hinkelammert, F. (2002) 'El sujeto negado y su retorno', in *Departamento Ecuménico de Investigaciones (DEI)*. Costa Rica.

Huntington, S. (2011) *The clash of civilizations and the remaking of world order*. New York: Simon and Schuster.

Kaes, R. (1993) *El grupo y el sujeto del grupo*, Amorrortu ed. Buenos Aires.

Kristeva, J. (2006) *This incredible need to believe*. Columbia University Press.

Martinez de, C., Ana, M. 'Reflexiones sobre las creencias, perspectiva desde el psicoanálisis y la epistemología genética', *Rev Psicoanalisis APA*, 76(4).

Martin Solar, A.M. (2019) 'Los comienzos del fanatismo', *Rev Psicoanálisis APA*, 76(4).

Meyer, T. (2001) *Identity mania, fundamentalism and the politicization of cultural differences*. London, New York: Zed Books.

Oz, A. (2011) *How to cure a fanatic*. Princeton University Press.

Paz, R. 'en Mesa redonda acerca de Creencias, ideales y certezas', *Rev Psicoanalisis APA Tomo*, 76(4).

Rubinstein, R. (2017) *Sports on the couch*. London: Karnac.

Rubinstein, R., y Halfon, M. (2011) Máscaras del fanatismo, paper presented in Argentine Psychoanalytic Association.

Sor Darío y Senet María (2010) *Fanatismo*. Buenos Aires: Paidós.

Chapter 4

New technologies, subjectivity, and addictive tendencies

There is no doubt that we are experiencing the consequences of a true revolution in many areas of our culture, which is going on throughout our planet. Various areas of human expression, transmission, learning, entertainment, and communication have been radically transformed, with a notable influence on our customs and habits, which have been mutating accordingly.

This revolution changed the spaces to be in solitude and the shared ones, the private and the public fields, the ways of getting "friends", "couples", and "followers", of becoming visible or staying hidden and even thus participate. It changed the ways of being "connected" or isolated from the rest of the world, the companion objects or fetishes that are taken everywhere and can be a source of security and protection. It changed the ways of being instantly informed, of locating and orienting oneself in unknown places, of restarting one's life, of trading, of moving money or goods, of summoning followers for different causes (political, social, defence of gender, recreational, etc.).

All these changes in doing, in power, and in being in the world have necessarily brought about many other changes in the constitution of our subjectivity. And this is even more noticeable for those who are "digital natives", who entered the cultural world with this baggage as part of that which surrounds them in their daily lives.

Those of us who work with the human soul, with its desires, longings, hardships, and those of us who practice clinical psychoanalysis have also seen how new forms of individual problems have been appearing, how certain psychopathological constellations or expressions have begun to prevail over others, and what are the predictions made about what will happen in next decades.

In this paper, I shall investigate several of these issues and try to find them on speculations extracted from the psychoanalytical theory and clinic in the course of my practice and my personal observation.

The subjective constitution develops through a process that begins with the first inscriptions of pleasure/displeasure, of presence/absence of the object of satisfaction. It starts from the original fusion and goes on to the

DOI: 10.4324/9781003293569-5

delimitation of a "not-me" and an "Ego", of an inside and an outside, of an anaclitical support in the need, to reach that plus of pleasure that precedes desire, love, and hate; from a precipitate of identifications to the shocks with which each libidinal stage will mark the evolution of subjects according to their culture and period.

As a structure open to the impressions and stimuli that come from the outside, the individual psyche is shaped by its relationship with the others around it, the providers of food and of both pleasant and painful stimuli. These others (who are, to a great extent, the parents) are bearers of imperatives, traditions, values, and demands typical of the culture in which they are inserted. The psychic constitution occurs in the interchange with these significant objects, which in turn carry with them models of eroticism, drive processes, affective states, ego possibilities, preconscious, and unconscious ideals. The subject-to-come looks himself or herself in the others, tries to find a unified image of himself/herself through them. In the course of this bonding with others, he or she builds up his/her ways of processing stimuli, his/her capacities to think and feel, his/her register of feelings, etc.

Inwardly, the encounter takes place between a perceptual apparatus that is gradually tied to representations which at first have the category of signs and then become meanings. These representations have sensory support in the visual and tactile fields (thing) and then in the auditory field (word). Each representation, together with the coenesthetic perceptions, will contribute to the correlated representation of a body (body image) convergent with the constitution of an Ego, a self.

This Ego, the arrival point of narcissism, unifies the fragmentation of previous phases, the autoerotic polymorphism. It also creates its own psychic face, different from the outside. It gives shape to a notion of space, of an interior and an exterior, which sustains the psychic processes of projection and identification.

We psychoanalysts have a set of models and theories to deal with how the process of humanization is produced in the interchange with the external environment, and how this impacts on the modes of perception, the transformation of signs into symbols, the quantity and quality of mental representations, feelings and affections, the tolerance to pain and frustration, etc. The construction of an "Ego", of a corporal image, is also going to be affected by all these processes, along with the vicissitudes of the libidinization, the erotic charges, and the desires. The way in which this Ego processes the stimuli, the marks left by the inscriptions of presence/absence, of pleasure/displeasure, the processes of identification, the image of oneself, the intrapsychic communication and the communication with others: all and each of the constitutive parts of this model are profoundly modified by the appearance of new technologies and the predominance of the visual.

We will ask ourselves what other psychic organization exists or what parameters are modified in the constitution of the subject in relation to that other captive of the screens, seeking to integrate contributions from other disciplines (communication theory, sociology) in order to articulate and enrich the psychoanalytic understanding of these phenomena.

We will take as an axis the subjective constitution to analyze how each of the processes that intervene in its formation vary with the current modes of technology and the visual predominance. All this will configure a different Self, a subject adhered to internal and external codes different from those of language, to another place in the social and communicative fabric, to other anchors of the principles of pleasure and reality. Some of its effects can be predicted by comparison with the model in force up to now, and others remain to be seen.

Let's take a first model where the subject is constituted and humanized in the (preponderant) bonding with another human being. This other decodes messages coming from the subject and gives them meaning. In this way, he/she allows the subject's emerging psychism to develop different functions and capacities. Another role of the object is to mediate between drive motions and bind them. It does this by nurturing the process of affective maturation, taking care of the perceptual thresholds so as not to expose it to non-metabolizable (traumatic) stimuli.

The intensity, speed, and quality of estimuli influence the way they are presented to the subject. These stimuli (or information packages) are multiple and heterogeneous. They will take on meaning for the subject as long as they are "libidinal information" and can be represented. The interaction with the object so that this set of multiple signals can acquire libidinal meaning is fundamental.

Representation is an act of cathexis or investment, linked to perception. There is a perceptive organization and then a perceptive knowledge in which pleasure/displeasure comes into play. Freud states that to perceive is to have a certain organization of the senses; the sense organs are able to inscribe a configuration to a certain extent. An encounter takes place between the biological perceptive system that structures it and the environment. As a result of this encounter, perception will give rise to a new order of realities. This is the perceptive organization.

In the process of approaching the world, the mark of pleasure/displeasure turns into a drive imprint (A. Green) which substantially influences the mode of perceptual organization, since it leads to perceptual knowledge, mediated by its inclusion. The preservation of the libidinal interchanges with the environment and the mother under the domain of the pleasure principle – which is in itself a representation, or the genesis of a representation, of affection – makes it possible to tolerate what is unpleasant and leads to the constitution of a purified pleasure-Ego that will permit to tolerate tensions and frustrations.

The purified pleasure-Ego is that which recognizes as its own the pleasant stimuli and projects the unpleasant ones. The economic principle that governs this structure is that of pleasure, and the goal of the self is the reduction of displeasure and the attainment of pleasure. This principle is enacted by the sexual drives. The Ego cathects perception, but the link with the perceived can consist of an introjection or an identification; thus, the object meets the Ego without differentiating itself from it. When the erogenous zones are "opened" (Maldavsky, 1988), a binding of these zones allows the constitution of a unified body-representation. For this, it is necessary that the external agent does not provide a contradictory stimulation – for instance, when the six-month-old baby is fed making him look through the window and introducing the spoon in his mouth when he is distracted.

Piera Aulagnier states that it is important to codify the movements of union or rejection (of the medium or the information). Those who investigate the mother-baby dyad pay attention to the thresholds of perceptual categories and the homeostatic and regulatory sleep/wakefulness and reciprocity/synchrony capacities, in order to observe the expression of pleasure/displeasure at a very early stage.

All these elements condition the perceptive knowledge, which as a minimum, must possess the qualities of similarity and difference.

Bion does not conceive thought as a cognitive process only but links it to the task of finding meaning and of providing meaning to an emotional experience. To make this possible, the capacity to tolerate frustration and mental pain in the process of one's own search for truth must be developed. Otherwise, the primitive elements within the mind will remain there as a kind of garbage or gravel, and will tend to be expelled in the form of somatizations, meaningless speech, fanatical ideas, or unhealthy group behaviours. On the other hand, the desire to know and approach the truth is painful and leads to avoidance of thought in order to escape suffering.

In Bion's two theories, thoughts appear at first in a rudimentary way, and afterwards a "thinking machine" is created whose function consists of transforming the set of primitive experiences, sensations, and perceptions into thoughts. In a second version, Bion advances the theory of the "container-content" emphasizing the emotional bond between mother and child and the role she fulfils with the baby, who experiences an accumulation of intolerable sensations and emotions that need to be expelled to the outside. The mother takes them, modifies and elaborates them within herself, and then returns them to the baby in a manageable way. By taking those thoughts already thought, the baby begins to organize within itself its own system of thought. Little by little, he or she will internalize not only the thoughts but the very function of thinking, which will enable him/her to digest and give meaning to his/her own emotional experiences. This is how psychic growth and development begin.

Other theories on perception also emphasize bonding. Spitz, who worked with blind subjects, proposed that there is a code to state what stimulus should be transformed into a significant experience (libidinal, cathected, symbolic) and into a coherent internal image (psychoanalytically, a mental representation) of the world. Of utmost importance for constructing this image of the world is the reciprocal bonding with the mother. In this climate of emotional dialogue, it is possible to gradually transform meaningless stimuli into significant signs (hence the importance of the object relation for the emergence of affects and of an organized perception).

In newborns, there is a coenesthetic organization (a globalized, primal, visceral intake system regulated by the autonomic nervous system) that manifests itself in the form of emotions. This phenomenon, called "reception", works like a binary system. On the other hand, in the subsequent development, there exists a diacritical organization where perception is carried out by means of peripheral sensory organs. It is localized, circumscribed, and intensive; its centres are in the cerebral cortex and its manifestations are cognitive processes, among which is conscious thought. Here knowledge is linked to the perceptive and thought processes, in which mental representations also intervene.

Clara Schejtman has studied some aspects of play in children. It is well known that many computer games encourage repetition. The most complex ones stimulate cognitive development (selection, anticipation, evaluation); they involve problem-solving, adaptation to complex and simultaneous stimuli, visomotor and special skills, enrichment of thinking at all levels. However, the practice of these games in detriment of less structured, recreational ones alters the transitional space (in which there are greater opportunities for the child's inventiveness) and leads to a form of adaptation similar to uncritical compliance (Winnicott).

Nowadays, children interact profusely with images as part of the reality presented to them, which diminishes the multiplicity of their own mental representations, compared to those coming from the reading of texts.

There might be a coagulation of senses rather than variability. This is manifested in children's growing tendency to assume that almost everything they observe is created by man in an artificial way, as if it is unthinkable that something may genuinely and spontaneously come from nature; as if what exists around them are also invented games. They confuse the material reality with the virtually created one.

Another referential scheme about perception is the one developed by Sami Ali. This author makes interesting contributions by analyzing the subject's relationship with his face. He affirms that the subject acknowledges that he/she has his own face, different from the others', and this results in a radical ambiguity: that of appropriating a face that begins to exist from the others' viewpoint.

Based on Konrad Lorenz's ethological works with the coral fishes, Ali affirms that the subject sees an other equal to him, and then, by sensory projection, separates an inside from an outside. Perception, he concludes, is a reflexive return on oneself. The outside (epitomized in the face) becomes thus occupied by a face capable of becoming an other: it no longer is one and the same thing with oneself. It is a projection that introduces a difference and a distance with respect to another "self".

The object of primary identification (the mother's face) coincides so perfectly with the subject's immediate field of vision that seeing and being seen, vision and the organ of vision, are at that stage indistinct. In front of the mirror, children do not see themselves as another, and they see another who is also himself/herself (they strip themselves of their self by imaginary duplication). Thus, they conceptualize the experience of the mirror as a disidentification of the maternal face followed by the identification with another face, which is their own.

Between these two moments, all the variants of perception take place, from the familiar as identical to the totally strange. With the introduction of the third term (the father), what the subjects perceive is one face (theirs) in relation to another, different from the mother's and also from their own. This opens the way to the identification of the body in its sexual difference.

Let's underline that there are many unresolved questions regarding the variations in the process of perception, in the inside-outside discrimination, in the binary or diacritic system, and its predominance, as a result of the exchanges children have with screens, with images and contents that emit signals, codes, messages, in a process of interaction very different from the one we have discussed so far.

The scopic

We have so far referred to perception since it encompasses all the sense organs.

The technological network leads to an abusive predominance of the visual over the rest, to an overload of the scopic. It seems appropriate then to include this perspective and review its impact on the subject.

The scopic drive is sustained in seeing. It is susceptible to fixation and it is also a drive focus whose expression is seeing, connected with perception by means of the visual organ, located in the eye.

Seeing is the expression of the eyes in their relationship with the object under consideration. Freud (in "Three Essays on the Theory of Sexuality") considers the drive to see one of the sources of child sexuality, together with the drive for mastery and cruelty. He made important contributions linking seeing with sexuality; he described a dialectic voyeurism/exhibitionism based on the perverts' pleasure of seeing understood as the fixation on provisional sexual goals prior to the sexual act.

Behind seeing is the judgement on sexual differences. In the history case of Little Hans and in the essay on Leonardo da Vinci, he will refer to the fetish as a substitute for the penis and to the role of castration in the scopic dynamics. The gaze becomes a theoretical operator whose bet is the enigma of the phallus and also the greatest effect of the Ego cleavage. The inclination to contemplate the particularities of naked sex is one of the original components of our libido.

In the relationship with the loving object, the optical impression is the way by which the libidinal excitement, stimulated by the attraction or beauty of that object, is most frequently awakened. There is also an apprenticeship in the interchange with that object, seeing it and touching it. The subject must try not to lose sight of that object that sustains him with its presence, and also that the object does not lose sight of him. By fixing the castration anxiety, the immobility of the image counteracts it and exorcises the primary separation anxiety.

In sensory terms, seeing relieves smelling, which is more archaic and quite near to touching. Seeing is like touching at a distance.

In the drive to see, there would be three phases: (a) to see one's own sexual organ; (b) to contemplate a foreign object; and (c) to be contemplated as an object by another person (to be seen).

Thus, in its active phase, the drive is a movement towards the object. Lacan states that the subject arises when being looked at by others. We must differentiate that visibility from exhibitionism or the loss of privacy (exhibiting what is private). This would be one way to be considered a subject instead of an anonymous user of the Web, as we shall see later.

Perhaps the "likes" of screens derive their addictive power from this narcissistic trap. Just as in the love life with an object, the subject is exposed and in the hands of that great other who must take him/her into account, who must have him/her in mind.

Representations

Let us now move on to the field of representations. The sensory imprints (signs) will be transformed into meaningful emotional experiences by the humanization the bond with the maternal object produces. This occurs through experiences of presence/absence, libidinal charge, increase and decrease of tensions, and pleasure/pain.

The thing-representations come with the signs; the others will constitute themselves linked to words. A certain number of them will remain in the preconscious, available for binding. The system of representations has a crucial influence on the constitution of the first images of oneself, as well as on the conscious and unconscious image of the body. The notions of "Ego" and "body" are then coordinated.

The representatives of drives, the categories of the seen and the heard (with their thing- and word-representations and the representational ordering of memory traces) collaborate in this constitution. We can find three kinds of representations: (1) Those related to the body form or scheme, related to the world of the exteroceptive and dependent on the sensory organs (perceptions and sensations). (2) Those related to proprioceptive sensations, associated to support, equilibrium, movement, hunger/satiation, tension/relaxation, cold/heat, and the diverse vicissitudes of pain. When linked to words, these sensations are transformed into affective feelings (fear, joy, etc.). They are lodged in the preconscious. (3) Those related to the erogenous zones, which give rise to desire. The latter begins with the decrease of drive tension, perceived as pleasure, and convokes the memory traces of satisfaction. The structure of desire establishes an intersubjective object relationship. Thus, the integrated erogenous body functions as a category of a semantic (that is, communicational) body, which issues and codifies bonding relationships.

The three kinds of representation are interrelated through the narcissistic organization of the self and the Oedipal fantasy organization, and they unify and integrate that way of functioning.

Piaget tells us that the mental image may be estimulated in different ways. Learning must take into account the uniqueness of each child's process of assimilation and accommodation, avoiding an excessive imitation or a level of compliance that becomes paralyzing.

Within the structure of the subject's desire, perceptions and representations will provide the ingredients for the development of the rest of the mental and psychical functions that are at the base of thought, cognitive processes, learning, imagination, fantasy, language, and communication, with all their accompanying affective nuances. In this way, what the subjects receive from their external environment as information is transformed into a cultural experience as long as they can develop a critical stance.

We can thus infer how relevant is the accompaniment of the adult in care for the child to metabolize, elaborate and, through the support and implementation of certain legalities, make the stimulation his/her own and give it his/her own direction and meaning.

Communication

In order to distinguish verbal and visual communication, with their differential effects, we may quote Humberto Eco (*The culture of the image and its relationship with singularity*), who in turn quotes Cohen Seat: "Verbal communication brings into play in the consciousness a semantic field that corresponds to evocations and affective connotations. The brain locates that desired meaning, excludes the others and thus generates the process of understanding".

Alain Touraine analyzes the mass culture and subjectivity with a sociological model. He proposes that an individual will become a subject only through the knowledge of an other with whom he works together to combine cultural memory with an instrumental project. Being a subject has to do with the construction of a self as an actor, with the desire to be one. This can only be achieved if there is a sufficiently large interface between the world of the instrumental action and the world of identity.

Vilches also compares, from the perspective of communication theory, the previous models with those that appeared lately. He quotes Habermas and Jakobson and their psychogenetic and sociogenetic theories. According to them, communication and memory are intimately related. We start with a psychic memory where linear sequences unfold in time. For communication to be possible, three conditions must be given: way of life, culture, and language. As bearer of a linguistic and cultural memory, the subject is a social actor. The psychic memory is socially expressed through communicative actions, realizing itself as speech, or acts of speech, which can be theatrical (subjective world), normative (social world), or conversational (objective world).

There is a psychic memory (immanent to language) and a cultural one, which is a psychic and a social register at the same time. These authors propose that communication is a constant play of speech acts, to the point that they define as social any act mediated by language. They define psychic memory as an immanent human faculty that is also a condition of any social memory.

We shall see how all this changes radically when the notions of user and network communication are introduced.

A new model

In the new model, typical of the image age, interaction takes place increasingly with objects/screens. The stimuli are predominantly visual, with a greater number of signals, a lesser number of absences, and a tendency to hyperpresence.

The lower regulatory incidence of the maternal object has consequences, whether for maintaining non-traumatic thresholds, processing signals, decoding them and giving them meaning, establishing an objective libidinal bond, etc.

While images allow the creation of some symbols, a significant amount of information remains unprocessed. Time is shorter and there is less contact with the object. The unprocessed information is less frequently linked to a meaningful content and what prevails is the tendency to communicate through signs.

In topical terms, this will lead to a thinner preconscious and a reduced availability of linkages with word-representations (Pierre Marty's scheme). The reduced predominance of the verbal will result, in turn, in a more prominent role of the corporeal and the action as means of expression of the psychic content. This diminished psychic inscription will alter the construction of the representational systems. For its part, the Ego will be restricted as regards the inscription of experiences of absence, cutting, or castration on the different levels.

In terms of interaction, there will be a lack of the essential affective support, both in quantity and in quality, so that the subject may become involved in culture patterns, its codes and legalities. These will be partially substituted by prefabricated or mimetic models provided by the images on the screens. Subjects will tend to identify themselves adhesively with those images and so to be massified, since they are the same for all the planet inhabitants who receive them. The voice, language, and actions of the characters, their clothes, and their ideology, are offered as archetypes for those who need something to sustain themselves with and are eager for objects. But they don't have the special, unique, and personal imprint of the bond with another human being in the mother/child dyad. The subject requires the presence of the object, which must be essentially satisfactory so that he or she can appropriate the stimuli, initiate processes of symbolization, and progressively assimilate the outside to his/her Ego. If subjects must adapt, or over-adapt, to the outside, it will be to the detriment of themselves, of the plasticity of their capacities and qualities, of their libidinal balance and homeostasis; and they will be eventually subjected to ideals that may make them suffer.

Their strength and ductility will be left in many cases with an orphanage of origin that will have a crucial impact as a deficit in the primary and secondary identification processes. In affective terms, this will translate into feelings of emptiness that account for the poverty, loneliness, and deprivation in which they find themselves. Tension and drive loading and unloading will often be repetitive, of poor quality and variety, all what the human object contributes with his/her times, nuances, and specificities.

This tendency to repetition is even more remarkable if we compare visual stimuli with those coming from reading and speaking, and the effect of this is a poorer development of the representational fabric. The maturation potential decreases; games tend to become compulsive, tending to pure loading and unloading, scarce elaboration and processing, and poor object communication. They do not help to structure or expand psychic layers and functions that are not directly associated with the game itself (such as memory and perception).

The affective qualities, the processes of imagination and fantasy are constrained in parallel with the screen proposals. Uniformity prevails over variability. There is a sort of coagulation of senses, as well as a distortion in the sense of reality: the material reality is confused with the virtual one.

Here are some examples. A nine-year-old girl, upon observing volcanic mud and geysers, far from being surprised by this beautiful phenomenon of nature, asked "who had turned on the game, who had put it on", and "when would it be put off". She could not conceive of the phenomenon outside of what was produced by virtual reality. A ten-year-old boy, observing some mummies in a museum, said he could not understand how tourists stopped to look at something that was false, invented. He only conceived of mummies as a trick in the movies.

But not everything is dull, flattening, and negative. If activities and games on screens alternate with moments of good object presence and bonding with the parental objects instead of supplanting them, one often observe the development of perceptive qualities, abilities, and talents, as well as quick and expert visomotor responses. In this universe of computer codes, the "sensitivity" to temporospatial patterns and to registers of shape and size, the discovery of new functions and applications, in other words, the capacity for invention is increased and coexists in a disparate harmony with the abilities promoted by the classical model.

Since the appearance of television, different authors (from psychoanalysis, social sciences, communication theory, and linguistics) have accounted for the modifications that occur both in the intrasubjective and intersubjective worlds, and this was accentuated in recent years with the invasion of the screens. In his work on the effects of TV on the psyche, José Sahovaler enumerates a set of them culminating in a "psychic flattening". There is perception without consciousness, with dissociated and unproductive fantasies and a recharge of the Pp-Cc system, as well as a regression to mere representation, with useless thoughts and attacks to the possibility of thinking. The real object's false independence increases the dependence on television. The image acts as a form of support and a way to sexual excitement, leaving the passive subject reduced to voyeurism, and it decathects the body.

This loss of human functions and attack on human capacities was examined by Umberto Eco, who stated that the mass media offered a homogeneous model, destructive of the cultural characteristics of each social group, and were aimed at an audience that unknowingly supports and suffers it. There is no effort to acquire a new experience; the experience is offered to passive subjects, uncritical with respect to what they receive. Symbols and functional myths reduce individuality to a minimum. The emotional, instead of being symbolized and represented, is induced and manipulated. Eco concludes that, as a means of mass control, media fulfil the same function that religious ideologies had in certain historical circumstances. They carry on the individual to a hypnotic and addictive state, leaving them with a false illusion of participation.

Many of these effects derive from the particularities of visual communication (a theme that Cohen Seat worked on and which was later taken up by C. Schejtman), governed by the right brain hemisphere (controlling vision and movement), which transmits the whole complex of emotions and their related meanings, but is unable to differentiate or discern. It forces to apprehend an undivided whole of meanings. Thus, the critical stance remains largely blocked. On the other hand, verbal communication, governed by the left hemisphere, brings into play in the consciousness a semantic field that corresponds to affective connotations. The brain locates the desired meaning, excludes others, and gives origin to the process of understanding.

The first model is the preferred one for advertising and is particularly useful during political campaigns. Focusing on the exercise of functions integrated to the social by the subject, both Eco and Touraine highlight the approach to cultural experience through the exercise of a critical function (numbed by the screens) as well as through the construction of the self as an actor.

The transience, speed, and immediacy of stimuli, and the loss of any social role, break the balance between the subject's symbolic capacity and the instrumental world. The subject thus loses his/her most precious attributes and comes close to being a zombie, a puppet.

This social level coincides with the structural, subjective change constituting the self that we spoke of when referring to psychic dynamics and organization.

The performative

In terms of language, effects correlative with all of the above are observed. Some linguists (such as John Austin) speak of a language "partition", arguing that languages include not only confirmatory but also performative statements.

In every statement, the two planes – the representative and the performative – operate more or less explicitly. Confirmatory statements are those which represent, describe or verify empirical facts. Performative statements, on the other hand, produce or "realize" facts.

Observing the advertising discourse, for instance, one can see that what is authorized is performative effectiveness: what is said is performed. Almost all descriptions have a prescriptive value. Language has this other aspect, in that it attempts to influence reality by the mere act of speaking.

In digital language, that of hypertexts and hypermedia, the emphasis is on its pragmatic, operative, and interactive dimension. It is a language that does by saying. In computer and digital language, this illocutionary dimension (Carlos Colina) is central. Hypertext links do not connect only contents scattered in different sites: they permit to jump from one communicative mode to another. It is possible to write a document, send an electronic message, participate in a chat with friends, be involved in a specialized forum, talk on the phone, listen to music or communicative activities, make calculations, program, create, or look up in databases. In addition – and this is essential for our discussion – the digital performative language has a self-referential value. The facts it produces are subjective ones (e.g., when saying "I congratulate you") and are subtracted from mere representative reality. They make the subject exist. This is the consequence of the commitment made by the mere fact of saying.

The Web creates a wide avenue for these modes of subjective presence to circulate, and does so permanently. It thus makes it easier for the subject to find himself and be found, seen, named by others. The performative thus acquires a fantastic validity, which together with other elements, boost the insatiable search of a presence and of the constitutive and constituting look of the subject at the moment of his/her inclusion, of his/her "click on".

This is also the reason for its great addictive power.

Digital communication

We think that computer language, and increasingly that which is realized by screens, tends to work in the way described. Changes in language accompany and produce effects on communication between individuals and groups. Experts in this area have remarked the disappearance of the category of the subject in network communication and its replacement by those of "user" or of node – a function in a network system. The user, whether as a sender, receiver, actor, or spectator, is an active part of the network. It is a functional device, both as an interactive node and as a data reservoir or memory. Communication takes place between the multipolar totality of integrated nodes; message flow and circulate according to the network codes and languages.

Who is the subject? Nobody, it does not exist as such in this system. The quality of the communication depends on the intelligence of the team. The participation of the subject does not affect it in the least.

Digital constructs, however, preserve cultural contents, are part of mass communication. They operate as devices in virtual transcontexts. But they bring important losses with them. One of them is referentiality. Jakobson states that every message is the bearer of its own reference. On the screens, where images and signs are virtual, they lose their referential load.

On the other hand, the signs exist there independently of any reality, beyond the evolution of time and space, that is, in an ahistorical time and in a space with no territory. This is totally opposite to what happens with acts of speech, which according to Habermas are true or false representatives and acquire legitimacy in the objective world.

All this has very important consequences for the subjects, who will suffer the destabilization of the referential systems with which they handled the verbal code and a de-realization of what they took for real, will see their conception of space and time altered and their notion of representation in crisis.

The connection with the cyberspace will force the subjects to adapt to new languages with a different regime of meanings. Their sensory and perceptual experience will also be modified, leading them to travel through an atopic, non-territorial space, where they will be presented to a vast series of virtual landscapes under visual or audiovisual form, static or in movement. According to communicologists (Derrida, Barthes, Van Dam, and Nelson, among others), the experience will be offered to them fragmented and discontinued; the new codes proposed to them will be those of the node, the nexus, the network, and multiple linearity, instead of those of the centre, the margin, the hierarchy, and linearity.

The subjects will depend on their capacity of adaptation, plasticity, and instrumental flexibility to get used to these new modes of bonding and their labour and technical needs. Their libidinal disposition will have to re-insert in the modes that this virtual and visual universe offers to the phantasmatic projections of their inner world, as well as to the possible satisfaction of their real objective needs.

In the previous era, the subjects were bearer of a memory, a knowledge, and a social and cultural network that marked and sustained them in social bonds allowing their interaction through acts of speech and communicative actions (Jakobson, Habermas). This situation had a definite psychic dimension, immanent to language.

The new technologies introduced a radical change. There are changes in the structures of representation at the social level: new forms of production, new services, new labour structures, and new ways of relating to others. Also, a new representation of time (in firms, work is accelerated as a result of the use of technology). The same happens with space as a consequence of economic globalization and the adaptation of places to accommodate technological elements. Also with the symbols, since the new technologies establish new symbolic forms which result in the use of a same language in the society as a whole – an information society ruled by speed, updating, effectiveness, and globalization.

Incompatibility between image and word

In psychic terms, this gap is widened by a marked incompatibility between image and word. This is quite evident in the history of psychoanalysis, from the first cases treated by Freud, particularly that of Anna O, where it was obvious how the stagnant libidinal quantity was an obstacle to language. Since his *Studies on Hysteria*, Freud sought to reduce with words (talking cure) the relevance of the images his patients brought up.

Being the hysterics mainly highly visual persons, when they put words to their suffering, images were diluted. When translated into words, the image was dismantled, as it were, and the patient was led to use another language. It could also be said that "the excessive presence of an unfailing gaze turns the scopic function into a dysfunction, and language, into words without a grammar" (Ritvo, 1990).

An example of these "words without a grammar" is what Freud described in Emmy von N.'s case history as "a mess in the head". Something similar can be said about the effect of screens on today's hyperconsumers: a jumble of saturation, confusions, anxieties, and nonsense.

Metapsychologically, the incompatibility of the scopic level with language implies

> "... tracing an erogenous edge that, when the drive returns to the subject's body, generates a closing effect and, in doing so, empties the gaze of its presence and reduces it to a leakage point located in the circuit of its moves. This relates, in turn, to the articulation between the drive and the unconscious".

(Ritvo)

Lacan maintains that what is looked at is what cannot be seen, and what is intended to see is the object as an absence (Seminar 11, "Partial Drive and its Circuit", chapter 16).

There is an equivalent incompatibility between the models and values on which the analytical praxis is based and those of today's culture. Psychoanalysis favours the oral and written word, time, waiting, space, in line with the processes and dynamics of psychic expression and elaboration; on the contrary, the current culture values the reified global image as much as the virtual one. Being seen is for it a synonym of being.

Subjectivity is presentified at the expense of a symbolic inconsistency that forces to compensate it with the body image, linked to the manifestation of sensations as an expressive mode, together with serious acting outs or discharges. The real is over-cathected by over-adapting to the ideals to which the individual adheres. Meanwhile, symptoms, which for psychoanalysis are the possibility of a change, from the perspective of culture are only the price to pay to achieve success.

Pornography

Fidias Cesio's work on pornography opens up another very interesting field for the understanding of sexualized visual effects on the psyche. The erotic charge that images and libidinal exchanges through the screens impose on the subject is undeniable.

Cesio states that the sexual charge that the observer's gaze places on the images, which have the nature of primordial hallucinations, brings with it the illusion of being the external objective "thing" that satisfies the need. To explain this, he quotes Freud in *The Interpretation of Dreams*: not finding the breast (object of satisfaction) that once satisfied his/her primordial need, the baby replaces it with its image, fully investing it with cathexes corresponding to the experience of frustrated satisfaction, which gives rise to a hallucination. What then is the hallucination? The presence of the image of the object of the objective reality, together with the illusion that in that image both hunger and libido are satisfied.

The primary fulfilment of desire is produced by trying to recapture the satisfaction through the hallucination. The affect invested in the image gives it the quality of the "real", to the point that it illusorily replaces the satisfaction of need.

Although in all cases of secondary fulfilment of desire, there is a hallucinatory participation, above all visual and experiential, this one derives from those ego processes of thought that allow the individual to foresee and anticipate things, thus tolerating waiting and frustration until the desire is fulfilled in the external objective reality.

The secondary fulfilment of desire is not total or imperious, as happens with the primary one. In the case of pornography, the images are such that they don't need any interpretation. They are monosemic, ahistorical, and current. They show everything in a realistic way and induce sexual excitement. Before them, the subjects are eagerly anxious, fascinated, and hallucinate. They contemplate the scene in the same way as they did with the primal scene, with no exclusions or glazes. They are narcissistically involved, identified with the protagonists, but at the same time are traumatically exposed to see everything without limits as their scoptophilia demands.

As happens with tactile eroticism, the eye plays here the role of an erogenous zone, as a kind of sense of touch at a distance. It is like touching with the eyes, in order to appropriate what is seen. It could be understood as the desire to look at an object in order to "feel close to it". This is what we observe in many children today, who look with the libidinal goal of feeling "close". It is a kind of appropriation of the virtually offered object, which is thus possessed in a flagrant denial of castration and absence. It feels like to be accompanied by the object that is not there and, at the same time, to dispense omnipotently with it, as if the object could be controlled and dominated at will.

On the other hand, many mothers leave their little ones, who are still bottle-feeding, in the presence of screens so that their baby feels accompanied and they may be free of their demands and claims of contact. In other cases, the baby is hypnotically attached to the screen and stares continually at it, ignoring the presence of the mother, father, or any other human being who wants to capture his/her attention. This behaviour, apparently paradoxical, is explained by the fact that humans can be with their children and not be at the same time, leaving them alone in frustration, while the screen is always there. The frustration that lies at the base of these constellations makes the baby look endlessly for that hallucinated object and bond, again and again, in an addictive way.

Finally, the use of new technologies triggers a series of other psychological effects and mechanisms: the immersion in the world of virtual reality in all its variants, the playfulness this world makes possible, the quality of the bonds formed through the interactions it provides, as well as its alarming addictive potential.

Virtual reality

The virtual world, the "handling" of the diverse technological applications, the games, videos, combinations of images, and so on, added to the skill achieved in games, chats, etc., produce a true massage to the Ego. The narcissistic pleasure derived from the practice of visomotor skills is added to the libidinal satisfaction coming from the involvement both in competitive situations (games) and in the search for contacts with which to interact, both through the "likes" and through comments and answers that increase the subjective presence and reinforce "one's being". We have already said that being seen is taken as an equivalent for being. Those who suffer from anguish and experiences of fragmentation or disintegration of the self find relief and refuge in networks through these mechanisms, and these experiences can be transformed into feelings of power and of an enormous capacity.

The daily reality, together with its pains, hardships, and duties, is replaced and evaded; the virtual space acts as a distraction or a pastime. Similarly to what happens with movies, theatre, concerts or musical recitals, dancing balls, or sporting and non-sporting games, their function is to put a distance, even temporary, from everyday reality. It is an immersion in another world, in another reality. These entertainments have the advantage of providing the psyche with a break, a moratorium, a kind of trip in which it momentarily strays away from worries and conflicts, and enjoys the vicissitudes of anything happening there. As a space to play, it reinforces the distance taken away from material reality. There is a withdrawal or return to a state of partial denial that turns it into a form of evasion. The playground is also a kind of transitional area. What happens there is real, it is temporally and spatially delimited, but to a certain extent, it remains isolated from the external reality. It is a kind of disconnection,

The game also generates a substitute libidinal satisfaction. In "Formulations on the two principles of mental functioning" (1911), Freud tells us that "fantasy is another psychic space where we witness the tendency of unconscious psychic processes to function according to the principle of pleasure, and to withdraw from what causes displeasure, denying or turning away from reality".

The energetic expenditure of repression is diminished or suppressed by freeing and discharging fantasies, and by treating as non-Ego parts, many contents found in or projected on the screens. In both ways, there is an important gain in pleasure and a withdrawal from oneself.

No less important is the denial of the passage of time (the hours spent in front of the screens are plenty) and of the increasing dependence and helplessness in the face of another human object. Staying for hours with the screens basically alters the presence/absence code. It leads the individual to a sustained hyperpresence in connecting with others through chats, groups, searches, or games. In this way, the subjects mainly counteract their experiences of loneliness and helplessness. They are never alone but always connected. They thus nurture the omnipotent illusion of always being with somebody, always included, and mitigate or maniacally deny the exclusion or absence. Their companion may be someone next to them or live in the most remote place on the planet. If this other is not there, he or she is feverishly sought out for chatting or to be included in some shared game.

In addition, the cell phone or screen (tablet, computer) is a companion that may be magically controlled or disconnected when the subject wishes. Either it is not exposed to the "normal" vicissitudes of the personal attachments or it tones them down. Being excluded from some bonds does not prevent the subjects from looking for many others. They rarely feel alone or abandoned, as is the case with face-to-face relationships of corporeal attachments.

Virtual attachments are of a different texture, as we shall see, but they also provoke emotions and sensations. As regards perception, we deem fully valid what Sami Ali has proposed with respect to the beginning of perception as a reflexive return, through the projective mechanism, which delimits initially an inside and outside. As Lorenz described with regard to the coral fishes, the Web users can see themselves in others, as anonymous as they are, thus initiating the discrimination Ego/other that allows them to perceive and constitute themselves at the same time.

The addiction

We can define an addictive behaviour by saying that it includes the consumption of some product or substance used to avoid any contact with the painful and to install basically pleasant experiences and sensations. A compelling need for the provided object or substance is established, whose absence progressively plunges the subject into a state of mental misery. This pushes him or her into a psychic and somatic dependence leading to repeated and continuous consumption.

Etymologically, "addict" comes from the Latin *ad dictum*, which means "without words". These subjects are not able to talk about their conflicting situations. They do not register them as such but as "an unmanageable compulsion that forces them to a discharge of a motor or hallucinatory kind, but not verbal" (H. Mayer). For them, words are devalued, they do not serve to communicate and even less to alleviate pain, although they do serve as an instrument of justification, manipulation, or cover-up. This is related to the fact that these subjects have not developed a representational world that could enable them to qualify their affective states. As we have pointed out, the incompatibility of the scopic with words, the communication through signs and images, and the foundation of subjectivity in the fact of being seen, facilitate the use of these codes by cyberaddicts.

In addicts, the bond with the maternal object reverts the child's dependence in such a way that he or she cannot find in it a safe framework to develop his or her experiences of satisfaction. This makes it difficult for them to form representations that may organize an internal mental object and enable them to have it present even in their absence. Their mothers are too present. Consequently, in addictive behaviour the ambivalent bond with that narcissistic mother is displaced, leaving no space for one's own experience, one's own subjectivity.

Significantly, this is what we find in screen addiction. Hyperpresence, with the alteration of the presence/absence register, is equivalent to the bond with the narcissistic mother. It seems to be the realm of the primary process, with a lack of registration of the passage of time (timelessness) and no need to submit to the ruling of the reality principle, of the true or the false.

The screen addicts' dependence can be measured by the number of hours spent in the virtual world. They have a compulsive and imperious need to subtract themselves from other realities of their daily lives, from whose "tyranny" they need to escape. Their eagerness to read the chats or any news that speak of them or mention them is intense. If there is none, they create it by sending messages or posting images on Instagram, Facebook, etc. Thus they ensure some response, some presence that may give consistency to their being in the world. It is as if they wanted "to be someone for someone". The others are indeed real, but they are often easily replaceable or interchangeable. As in other addictions, we observe here that when there is no consumption or connection, the syndrome of abstinence settles down: intense anxiety, restlessness, boredom, worry, irritability, aggressiveness. When contact is reestablished, when plugged into the appliance, calm reappears.

In substance addicts, the chemical effects (particularly at the brain level, with their vast sensory impacts) are crucial in their search for consumption. In cyberaddicts, although there may be chemical stimulant effects, these come from the release of endogenous amines (noradrenaline, dopamine, etc.) through pleasant Ego experiences. It is precisely this chemical effect that has been mentioned by the most important social network companies (e.g., Facebook) in several newspaper articles when admitting the negative consequences of its manipulation on a global scale (two billion users per month). These articles acknowledged a particular kind of exploitation. In *The psychology of being liked on social media*, Sean Parker (2017) described the system of users posting content and receiving likes as

> … a social-validation feedback loop … exploiting a vulnerability in human psychology… We need to sort of give you a little dopamine hit every once in a while, because someone liked or commented on a photo or a post or whatever. And that's going to get you to contribute more content, and that's going to get you … ever more likes and comments.

And Start Digital executives express:

> If you're like any of the Start Digital team, then one of the first things you'll do in the morning is check your social feed. Depending on

your poison of choice, it could be Facebook, Instagram, Snapchat or Linkedin. Whichever platform we're on, one of the first check points is the 'notification' tab. 'Has anyone liked something of mine'? 'Has anyone tagged me'? etc., etc. It's a habit we quickly get pulled into. It's addictive. Have you ever stopped to wonder why it's so addictive?

That little rush you get when your post gets more 'likes' than normal? There is a reason for it: dopamine. For every thumbs up or heart we get a little psychological high through a shot of dopamine. The more 'likes' the more shots. The more shots we have, the more shots we want. And we're in a loop. Scientists used to think dopamine was responsible for pleasure in the brain, but we now know that rather than create pleasure it makes us seek it.

Although in the advertising media, the dopamine genesis of screen addiction is taken as the main cause, they adhere to an extremely reductionist and limited biological model, which obviously skimp on a deep analysis of its cause in subjectivity and bonds.

A sort of elation, then, is experienced that stimulates the presence, power, omnipotence, and self-control of the subject. Its sources, as mentioned, are varied: the weakening of the repressive mechanisms and the acting out of fantasies; the multiple negations of the dependence on the object, of the passage of time and of the absences, as well as of the ruling of material reality; the possibility that the subject be included or not at will. The individuals feel capable of seeing, touching, and disposing of everything they want, almost without limit. On the contrary, everything connected to frustrations, absences, painful affections, and helplessness tends to be momentarily suppressed from the register of sensitivity.

These intense sources of pleasure, in turn, mobilize an insatiable greed, where what is seen is confused with the thing itself, as in pornographic images. This leads to the endless repetition of such images, since the inherent and basic frustration never disappears.

Also to be noted is the almost disappearance of the "down time", that in which an encounter with some other human being is expected, whether in a waiting room, on a trip, in a café, etc. There is no waiting, there is no down time, because the magic presence of the screen occupies and gives life to that time where "nothing happens". The paradox is that the subject is then captured, imprisoned by the images and "down to death" to connect with other realities.

Bonding quality

For some authors (e.g., Fischbein), there is a way of bonding with the object that is typical of addicts. It is an asymmetrical relationship in which the subject urgently needs to merge with the object, so that it obfuscates and alleviates its inner emptiness, its intolerable feeling of "not being". It is not an "object of desire": it is an object deeply needed and desired to calm and conjure up boredom, discomfort, anxiety, and to provide the self-esteem that the individual is unable to give and keep for himself (Kohut). When he succeeds, he manages to calm down.

Lewkowicz (quoted by Fischbein) argues that the subject is determined and shored up largely from the outside, and is constantly aware of how he or she is seen and how his/her image is defined by the environment, since it is there where his/her fragile self-esteem is sustained and supported.

In our days, we observe that each "like", each response to an interaction in any social network, provides its grain of presence and of self-esteem. Even provocations and negative comments meet that condition. The point is to be, to be taken into account, to generate "something" in someone else. However, the models of the screens, as objects imposed from outside on an anonymous mould, do not respect the uniqueness of each subject, their particular traits and characteristics. In order to do so, they would have to face their own imperfections and incompleteness and tolerate them, which entails to mourn their own uniqueness.

These individuals cannot do that: they have difficulty in grieving because of their narcissistic resistance. "The object is always kept alive, despite attempts to declare it dead. It is this what attempts against the psychic elaboration" (Stisman). Besides being always alive, the object is always ready, always at hand: it is enough to make a click in order to have it for one, and another click to disconnect. The subject will never be exposed to the other not being there (unless his/her gadget is not charged or out of order and needs to be urgently replaced).

The experience of mastery and control of the object is thus strongly reinforced, and with it, the feeling of esteem and power. This "drug" is difficult to obtain in the life of relationships with another non-virtual one, since it imposes times, pauses, alternations, absences, nuances, contrariness, and oppositions. The suffering and frustration coming from others is amortized and fades away illusorily as long as this effect lasts. On the other hand, in adults, more and more memories, contacts, projects, plans, unstorable stories are accumulated. They are considered very valuable objects, since "they have everything", in allusion to the increasingly vast movements and resources of their daily life. Not in vain, technology has invented the "clouds", virtual places that guard those pieces of the subjects' lives, and protect them against their possible losses.

Bibliography

Aulagnier, P. (2003) *The violence of interpretation. From pictogram to statement.* London: Routledge.

Bion, W. (1984) *Learning from experience.* London: Routledge.

Bion, W. (1967) *Second thoughts, selected papers on psychoanalysis.* W Heineman Ed.

Cesio, F. (2003) 'Reflexiones sobre la pornografía y transferencia', *La Peste de Tebas*, 28.

Colina, C. (2002) *El lenguaje de la red, hipertexto y posmodernidad*. Caracas: Universidad Católica Andrés Bello.

D'Alvia, R. (1995) 'El cuerpo en psicoanálisis', in *Revista de Psicoanalisis*. APA, N 4.

Eco, H. (2000) *Apocalypse postponed*. Indiana University Press.

Fischbein, J. (2007) 'Los vínculos Adictivos', *Revista de Psicoanalisis*. APA, T 64, N 4.

Freud, S. (1905) *Three Essays on the theorie of sexuality*, standard ed., Vol VII.

Freud, S. (1911) *Formulations on the two principles of mental functioning*, standard ed., Vol 4, 91.

Green, A. (2005) *Key ideas for a contemporary psychoanalysis, misrecognition and recognition of the unconscious*, Routledge.

Haimovich, E. (1992) 'Sujeto y eficacia performativa del lenguaje', in *en Super Yo y Filiación, Destinos de la transmisión*. Laborde Editor Amorrortu.

Lacan, J. (1988) '(Pulsión parcial y su circuito Cap 16, seminario 11) Jacques Lacan', in *An annotated bibliography*, Vol 1. Routledge.

Laurent, A.P. (2003) 'La pulsión escópica y sus destinos, en La Mirada y La Voz', in – *Lecciones Psicoanalíticas*, Nueva Visión.

Lewkowicz, I. (1998) 'Subjetividad adictiva: un tipo psicosocial históricamente instituido', *Rev. Asociación Argentina de Psicología y Psicoterapia de Grupo*, T 21(1).

Maldavsky, D. (1988) Estructuras narcisistas, constitución y transformaciones Amorrortu.Editores.

Marty, P. (1993) *La Psicosomática del adulto*. Amorrortu Editores.

Mayer, H. (2000) 'El sostén interior', *Revista de Psicoanalisis*. APA, T 57, N 1.

Ritvo, J. (1990) 'Incompatilidad de la palabra con lo escópico', *Conjetural*, abril N 20.

Parker Sean Sean Parker unloads on Facebook: n.ov 2017 "God only knows what it's doing to our children's brains" (axios.com).

Sahovaler J. (1998) *Psicoanálisis de la televisión*. Ed. El Otro, Bs As.

Sami, A., C, R., cuerpo Imaginario, P. (1996) capítulo sobre Narcisismo. Paidos Editorial, chapter on Narcissism

Schejtman, C. (2017) 'Los juegos del niño en la actualidad', *Su incidencia en la estructuración del psiquismo*, UBA, Facultad de Psicología, Publicaciones.

Sorrentini, A. (2003) Pornografía, en, La Peste de Tebas, N 28.

Spitz, R. (1965) *The first year of life*. New York: International University Press.

Stisman, A. (2006) 'Obstáculos en la cura: los vínculos adictivos' Paper presented in APA, Cientific Activity.

Touraine, A. (2009) *La mirada social. Un marco de pensamiento distinto para el siglo XXI*. Barcelona: Paidos.

Vilches, L. (2017) *El lenguaje en los medios de comunicación*. Madrid: Ed. Dykinson.

Winicott, D. (1971) *Playing and reality*. London: Tavistock Publications.

Chapter 5

Pandemics

We are going through a unique experience in the history of mankind. Two billion six hundred million people, one-third of the planet's human population, have experienced the consequences of changes and restrictions in their daily lives as a result of measures taken in all nations in response to the threat posed by the spread of the coronavirus. Never before has there been such a worldwide reaction to an event. We could perhaps compare it to the glaciations from 2400 to 400 million years ago that caused migrations, death, and extinction of species. This is an experience of large human masses, which makes it possible to analyze their reactions and observe the similarities and differences according to cultures, systems of government, and geographical particularities. Speculatively, it may be tempting to homogenize mechanisms or behavioural patterns that have a common triggering factor; however, the results and paths are diverse.

As antecedents, and obviously on a smaller scale, we have the responses to other plagues or pestilences that devastated major population groups. It is worth mentioning the plague of Athens in 430 B. C.; the Antonine plague in Rome in the 2nd century A.C.; the Justinian plague in the Byzantine Empire in the sixth century; the bubonic plague in Europe in 1346, and the epidemics of yellow fever, Spanish flu, polio and AIDS in more recent years.

Cinematographic fiction, for its part, made multiple approaches both to biological plagues and to the dangers suffered by humanity in the form of large-scale natural disasters (tsunamis, earthquakes, hurricanes) or invasions by beings from other planets.

Finally, the examples of global conflagrations and their consequences on our species also offer food for thought.

Recently, physicist Stephen Hawking warned of what he saw as several threats to humanity, pointing to "low-probability, high-impact events such as asteroid collisions with the Earth, and others such as artificial intelligence, climate change, genetically modified viruses and nuclear war".

The threat posed by the virus and its effects on human beings gave rise to a search for ways of defending ourselves, attacking or avoiding its harmful

DOI: 10.4324/9781003293569-6

and/or lethal repercussions. The lack of preparation for such a circumstance puts us in a disadvantageous situation with traumatic characteristics.

In psychoanalysis, much work has been done on the concept of trauma in terms of the psychological response to disruptive situations for the subject, including quantitative elements (the magnitude of the trauma), the previous state of the subject (ego integrity), his/her disorganizing responses, the loss of continuity (there is always a before and an after), the subject's defenceless and helplessness, as well as the possibilities of recovery or working through.

On this occasion, we are faced with an event that threatens the survival not only of subjects but also of the species to a large extent, and we cannot think only of individual traumas but also of general responses.

In the present context, a set of factors transform the modes of daily and "normal" or habitual reaction of individuals and make them function with the characteristics enunciated by Freud in "Group Psychology and Analysis of the Ego". This modality, which we could call "regressive", leads them to experience and behave in more archaic and primitive ways.

This "mass" functioning arises as a result of: (1) a situation of crisis or threat to humans as a whole (pandemic), (2) one of whose components, fear, is enhanced by the mass media (radio, newspapers, TV) as well as by the global use of digital technology, and (3) the intervention of the State as guarantor and controller of the situation, altering the government/subjects power equation. Some significant phenomena observed are the total obedience to authority and the passivity of the masses.

Characteristics of the masses

Their members are held together by libidinal ties with each other and with the leader, as well as with a set of values and ideals they share and cultural productions and conditions that give them their identity mark (city, region, country). They may respond in a cohesive or dispersed manner, but their lack of rational and critical thinking is notorious.

Likewise, there are masses with an active behaviour and others with a passive one. In active masses, individuals acquire feelings of power that allow them to surrender to their instincts. Moral conscience disappears as well as the feeling of responsibility, repressions are thrown away. The individual has the spontaneity, the savagery, the enthusiasm, and the heroism of primitive beings.

The mass is impulsive, fickle, and excitable. Guided almost exclusively by the unconscious, nothing in it is premeditated. It does not tolerate any delay between what it desires and its realization. It has a feeling of omnipotence where the idea of the impossible disappears.

The current situations of social distancing and the confinement in the house strongly predispose to a passive mass behaviour. Indeed, the conformation of active masses of any sign (protests) is considered extremely dangerous because it favours the risk of contagion and therefore is punishable and reprehensible.

We must consider the unconscious dynamics that sustain the social functioning of the individuals integrating the masses in each country and region. Between each and every one of them, a libidinal link is generated through the processes of identification and the community of situations and feelings that bind them together. This creates a link with the leader, and also, in this case, with the slogans of care and protection of life that emanate from the authorities. In this situation, the hypnotic effect and the group suggestibility have a strong influence. The mass is influential, credulous, and uncritical. It thinks in images, as it happens in free fantasizing. Their feelings are simple and exalted. There are in it no doubts or lack of certainty. To the same extent, it does not care about the truth. Desire predominates over reality. And the greatest longing is for survival, the preservation of oneself and of loved ones.

To influence the mass, it is not necessary to present logical arguments, but to paint the most vivid images, to exaggerate, and to repeat the same thing many times. There is a tendency to transform the suggested ideas into actions, as if speaking to an automaton without will.

The stimulus of fear thus operates as a universal and effective trigger.

Some conceptions of bonding provide another perspective on it. R. Kaes states that conscious and unconscious contracts and alliances are present in every bond. The latter are intrasubjective formations built with the purpose of reinforcing in each subject the needed narcissistic and object cathexes, while at the same time reach agreements regarding what will be rejected, denied, or excluded. The place of each person in the group obliges him/her to sustain such pacts and alliances, which in turn demand obligations, subjections, psychic costs and benefits, and entail gratifications. One fundamental form of unconscious alliances is the narcissistic contract, whereby the subject is assigned a function and a place by a discourse that exalts ideals and values, and which transmits the culture and certainties of the social group. This contract is articulated with the so-called "pact of denial", which describes the operations of repression, denial or negation, disavowal, rejection, or entrenchment that, in any intersubjective bond, are required for the bond to be constituted and maintained. This agreement ensures the continuity of the investments and benefits they bring to the bond and obtain from it. There are two polarities: one, organizing the bond and the intersubjective space, and the other, defensive of the internal, intrapsychic space. The psychic reality of couples, groups, families, and institutions is sealed on such alliances.

In the present pandemic, the virus has been catalogued as the "enemy" with which one is at war. By virtue of its potential threat, the possible carriers of COVID – the inhabitants of localities or regions where it is most widely circulating – are encompassed by the "psychic infection" (in addition to the biological one) of contagion, which reinforces the narcissistic contracts and pacts of denial of the "clean" or virus-free places inhabitants. Many communities shut themselves in defence of their health, strengthening their bonds of belonging in a manner similar to what happens in wars with the feeling of national identity.

The potential carriers of the contagion are denied, rejected, and deemed dangerous, are not allowed access to those territories, and even treated as if they were stripped of their status as fellow human beings. Besides, intolerance and hatred disappear within these groups. As long as the plague lasts, individuals behave as if all of them were homogeneous; they tolerate the specificity of the others, consider themselves their equals, and do not feel any repulsion towards them. This narcissistic restriction is produced by the libidinal attachment to members of the same group. Contagion is of a hypnotic type: every act and feeling is contagious. The suggestibility is similar to that of hypnosis: as the suggestion is identical for all, reciprocity is increased. All negativity is massively projected onto outsiders.

This hypnotic infection by suggestion also makes it possible to understand the displacement of the category of "murderer", comparable to the virus vector of death, with which careless subjects or those who defy preventive measures with their behaviour are labelled. Many of them are verbally and physically assaulted by their peers and neighbours.

With many medical professionals and other health agents (nurses, assistants), a paradoxical attitude is adopted. On the one hand, they are publicly praised and applauded for their selfless work in helping the affected by the virus – as those who embody socially recognized values and ideals (such as sacrifice and struggle for the sake of others' health) – but, on the other hand, an attempt is made to expel them from their homes for being "dangerous". This double inscription can be explained by the clear division of categories between the (distant) social ideal and the (dangerous and close) neighbour.

The media

In this pandemic, the media – mainly TV news channels, as well as digital technologies (computers, cell phones) – had a central role through their information and WhatsApp messages sent from family members and chains of friends or groups of belonging, disseminators of both true news and fake news. With individuals deprived of direct interpersonal, body-to-body contact, these messages were the channel through which the entire flow of information and communication could largely circulate in a massive way all over the planet. Their capacity to influence the masses and generate emotional states, thoughts, and actions played a major role. It is important to analyze their significant impact on the psyche, not only because of information itself but also because of what was said, the amount of it and in what way was it transmitted, and what was masked and remained hidden.

These information packages have been different and variable in each country. However, the common element of fear, conveyed by the numbers of dead and infected people, images of cemeteries, body bags, graves, intensive care units, has prevailed over warnings, videos or prevention and explanatory programs on how to act in the face of danger.

The communication by images activates circuits of the right cerebral hemisphere that lead to an overall grasp, with high emotional voltage and little critical and elaborative function. On the other hand, the subject tends to identify adhesively with the proposals, messages, mandates, and prohibitions disseminated by communicators and representative leaders, and to become subsumed into the mass. These communicators and leaders offer themselves as archetypes of care and the common good for those who need them, isolated and avid for love and objects which could support them. The affective qualities, the processes of imagination and fantasizing are reduced in parallel to the proposals of the screens. There is an increased tendency towards uniformity, instead of variability.

The image serves as a support and an element of sexual arousal, and the subject becomes a passive voyeur, so that the corporeal and the contact with the other are further decathected. It tends to provoke a psychic flattening, where the emotional, instead of being symbolized or represented, is induced and manipulated. Highly functional symbols and myths reduce individuality to a minimum. Referring to the mass media, Humberto Eco stated that their proposals offer a homogeneous model, which fulfils for the control of the masses the same function that religious ideologies had in certain historical periods. They lead individuals to a hypnoid and addictive state, which tends to detach them from the reality that surrounds them.

A bit of history

In order to understand some of the processes that are currently occurring as a result of the pandemic, it is necessary to delve a little into the knowledge and history of the subject/government relationship.

In the pre-modern period, kings, emperors, and feudal lords were masters and lords of rights and wills, occasionally sharing their power with religious representatives. From the 15th and 16th centuries onwards, the national state emerged as the political organization of modernity. The national state as an institution came to rule and condition the life and actions of the inhabitants of a territory through an entity, the government, which was responsible for the administration of the state. The political actions it undertakes will ideally be organized in favour of the "common good" or the "public interest" of society as a whole. The State is a power structure exercised through institutions (Justice, Armed Forces, etc.) and officials who carry out the required activities. Conceptually it is built under the idea of sovereignty, and monopolizes coercion, the creation of norms and codes, tax collection, and economic administration. In the exercise of their power, State officials (particularly those in the executive branch) make decisions in various situations through actions defined as political. Each society, each State and each government has its own interests, perspectives, and culture on how to deal with its problems as well as on the legitimate modes of citizen participation in public affairs.

The emergency situation caused by the pandemic substantially alters the subject/government relationship in all countries. The rights and powers of one or the other unbalance the power relations in favour of the State. The "reason of State" has its antecedent in Machiavelli's statement: "In deliberations in which the salvation of the homeland is at stake, no consideration should be given to what is just or unjust, what is pious or cruel, what is praiseworthy or shameful, but, leaving aside any other respect, one should follow that path which saves the life of the homeland and maintains its freedom". Later, Giovanni Botero and then Carl Schmitt, starting from a similar concept, understood, legalized, and justified the advance of the power of the State over the liberties and rights of all citizens when there were reasons that demanded it. In this sense, the reasons of State are predominant, and the sacrifice of oneself and others for the sake of something superior (war, epidemic, crisis) is imposed. Schmitt will question himself under Nazism, postulating that the real sovereign is the one who decides the exceptional situation. It is what is called decision-making; it is the one who has the capacity to decide on the relationship with war. The only true leader, the only important skill for this great leader is to be able to carry the discourse of the exceptional who engages in war.

The reason of State today consists in avoiding the contagion of the populations by this quickly and easily propagated virus, with its sequel of deaths, particularly in the most vulnerable sectors (the elderly, people with previous illnesses). Each government must ensure the care and prevention of the health of the population under its responsibility. Likewise, it needs to prevent the health system from being overwhelmed by the care of serious cases and be accountable for negligence or mismanagement that may increase the number of deaths. The political costs paid for the government if the quality of this kind of management is not fair are undeniable.

In Argentina, the exercise of such duties is mediated by officials whose suitability, preparation, capacity, and political interest are highly variable and fickle, and who depend on the diverse and sometimes opposing criteria with which they manage their areas, regions, or municipalities. Decisions on "giving relief from disaster" prevail over other spheres of daily life, such as economic activity, work, schooling, recreation, travel and meeting possibilities, and the transit and mobility of people. In this way, the living conditions, duties, and rights of the inhabitants of each territory are suspended, and each individual's will and freedom are restricted and subjected to the discourse and exercise of power by those who undertake the care and custody of the whole.

To understand the mechanisms and actions implicit in power chains, it is interesting to know Michel Foucault's contributions. According to this author, power establishes relationships between subjects who make up, in some way, an association or group; and to exercise it, training techniques, domination procedures, and systems to impose obedience are used. The strategies employed are surveillance, reward, punishment, pyramidal hierarchy, etc. The power relationships seek that the dominated subjects perform the desired behaviours; that is, it incites, induces, diverts, facilitates, expands, or limits certain behaviours. And it is always carried out over free people and is capable of affect their decisions.

In this case, we observe, on the one hand, the adoption of restrictive and punitive measures "for the good of the majority" and the punishment and conviction (prison sentences, economic fines) of those who attempt to defy such rules. The state of emergency, with its social and legal backing, enables punitive acts to be carried out. This occurs both at the social level (justice, police) and at the individual level, with verbal and corporal attacks on those who are considered guilty, offenders; in short, enemies. The categories of friend and enemy quickly polarize the whole in a way that is totally comparable to what happens in a state of war. On the other hand, fear and prevention campaigns become an important part of the public scene through most of the mass media, which permanently provide profuse information on the progress and evolution of the pandemic.

Obedience to authority and passivity of the masses

To understand how millions of people around the world support and endure very important restrictions to their usual life for an indeterminate period of time without major expressions of rebellion, violence or chaos and disorganization, at least so far, it is useful to recall Stanley Milgram's experiments on obedience to authority.

This American psychologist from Yale University set out in 1963 to measure the willingness of participants to obey the orders of an authority even when they might conflict with their conscience. The research team had to persuade participants to apply painful electric shocks to other subjects (who were simulating actors). Many continued to deliver the shocks despite the actor's requests and pleas to stop.

This study followed the trial and sentencing of Adolf Eichmann for crimes committed against humanity during the Holocaust by the Nazi regime. Were there a million accomplices who just "followed orders", as Eichmann declared?

Milgram arrived at two main hypotheses: there was conformity and there was reification. They are summarized in this paragraph: "Having no aptitude or knowledge for decision making, especially during a crisis, the subject transfers it to the group and its hierarchy. The group is for each person the model of behavior. [...] The essence of obedience lies in the fact that persons consider themselves as the instrument for the fulfillment of others' desires, thus ceasing to be subjects who are responsible for their actions. Once this transformation in the way of perceiving the situation has occurred, all the essential characteristics of blind obedience occur". Milgram cites as an example the respect of soldiers for their superiors: the former obey and execute instructions and orders dictated by the latter, through which they delegate the responsibility and consequences of their actions to the hierarchy.

Coincidentally, Freud considered the Army and the Church as models of an artificial mass that shares the illusion of having a boss present, a paternal substitute who watches over the care of the whole, loves them all equally, and at the same time keeps the mass united. This libidinal model also preserves from the experience of anguish and panic due to the rupture of affective bonds. The fusion with the mass relieves the subjects from using their critical thinking and from making autonomous and responsible decisions; these decisions are deposited in the one who commands, for better or for worse, the destinies of the rest.

Past and present references give an account, with different approaches, of this current characteristic of the masses in different parts of the world. In *The Origins of Totalitarianism*, Hanna Arendt explained the unwavering adherence to demagogues in populist movements. She found there atomized subjects whose thought was obstructed by artificiality, with spaces in which an only truth occupied the place of knowledge. This, said Arendt, is articulated with a public sphere where information and alternative meaning systems are perfectly coherent, and what is offered are not facts (not even invented ones) but the impossibility of establishing a difference between factual truths and opinions. She asserted that only factual information guarantees that we can pronounce on something with an anchor in reality. Otherwise, there are only states of mind but not opinions. For this author, the absence of certainties does not free us from the responsibility of caring for the world we share.

There is currently a breakdown in the public space, derived from the enormous power of networks and digital technology. The emotional charge is manipulated to expel dissident voices and fill the possible debate with affective overtones of fear, illusion, etc.

Giorgio Agamben, for his part, questions the concept of "social distancing". He states that "the current health emergency can be seen as the laboratory where the new political and social structures that await us are being prepared. The new digital technologies have long made it possible to communicate quite properly at a distance. Let us discuss the singular phenomenon produced by the measures of social distancing. These measures, together with panic, have undoubtedly created a mass, but inverted (according to the concept expressed by Canetti in *Masses and Power*), made up of individuals who keep at all costs distanced from each other. This mass is not dense but dispersed and remains a mass if we define it by its uniformity and passivity, in the sense that in no way would it be possible for it to carry out a truly free movement. It expects to be conducted by a leader. It is a mass based on a prohibition, but precisely for this reason, is particularly compact and passive". Agamben is surprised by "the ease with which a whole society has accepted to feel plagued, to isolate itself at home and to suspend its normal living conditions, its working relationships, friendship, love and even religious and political views. Why was there no opposition and protests, as was certainly possible to imagine and as usually happens in these cases? Hypothesis: because the plague was already there" – referring to living conditions. For Agamben, the collapse of all common convictions and faith is evident. "Humans no longer believe in anything except bare biological existence, which must be saved at all costs". Apropos of this, he quotes Montaigne: "We do not know where death awaits us, so let us wait for it everywhere. To meditate on death is to meditate on freedom. He who has learned to die has unlearned to serve. Knowing how to die frees us from all submission and all coercion".

It is clear that the human masses as a whole have so far accepted the imposed measures and restrictions in a totally passive way. Control and care are once again deposited, in an almost totalitarian and absolute manner, in the hands of those who hold political power. This fact, which is happening on a global scale, is unprecedented. Although many measures are taken with the advice of specialists in infectious diseases, public health experts, the WHO, and the bearers of discourses and places of knowledge validated by this political power, people live as if they were in a state of war in which the threat to life and survival becomes the enemy.

In this context, the absence of a spiritual or religious discourse is striking. Would such a presence be necessary? It could be anticipated by some media discourses calling the current state of affairs an apocalypse, an end of the world. It is as if "the religious need, which the church is no longer able to satisfy", suggests Agamben, "groped for another place to establish itself and found it in what has in fact become the religion of our time: science. This, like any religion, can produce superstition and fear or, in any case, be used to spread them".

This phenomenon of the absence of any religious leadership during the present pandemic is certainly novel. Science has tried to exercise such leadership, but resorting to elements and models derived from mystical religious thought. The latter is characterized by offering magical explanations, by the belief in a superior or natural power that is behind the causation of all phenomena. There would be a war between God and Satan in which we are mere pawns. All explanations ultimately refer to a struggle between Good and Evil, and then it is translated this into its political correlate. It could be said that the belief in conspiracy theories as the cause of the pandemic (the laboratories, the FBI, the Chinese) is a secularized version of that theological-mystical conception.

Finally, quoting Zizek, does this epidemic make any sense at all? "What is really difficult is to accept the fact that the epidemic is the result of pure contingency", he says.

Rituals that organize identity: time

The quarantine measures imposed on populations as a way of avoiding the spread of contagion by the virus have been and are in many cases longer than the 40 days that their name indicates. In Argentina, for example, they have been in place for more than a year in varying degrees. These measures imply restrictions and changes in daily life aimed at minimizing interpersonal contacts. They range from almost total and absolute confinement at home to a certain degree of openness and variable and regulated contact in virtually all areas.

Its application had effects on bodies, minds, and social ties, a real impact because of the rupture and breakage of daily life, with disorganization and the need to readjust to the new conditions. The life we lead on a daily basis is full of rituals, habits, and customs that play an organizing and stabilizing role in our psyche. They are part of a silent and invisible support of our being.

We are ourselves, we recognize ourselves, and we are seen and recognized by others thanks to a combination of elements that give us a sign of identity. Our body, the social and affective bonds we establish (family, couple, friendships, work), the places we inhabit, the values and ideals we share, language, music, clothes, typical foods, etc., even if they undergo changes and shocks throughout our lives, carry the experience of "being in the world" and have as a correlate to sustain us, strengthen us and provide us with a certain degree of coherence and self-esteem. L. and R. Grinberg state that, beyond the structure, the bond, the feelings, the fantasies, or the body (being seen by others or by oneself), identity is a concept that includes three kinds of integrations: (1) spatial integration (which establishes a relationship between different parts of the self and the bodily self, provides cohesion and allows to contrast it with objects; (2) temporal integration (which encompasses the different representations of oneself over time, generates continuity between them and lays the foundation for the feeling of selfhood, and (3) social integration (the self in its relationship with surrounding objects, which generates feelings of identification and of belonging). In each individual's evolution, the feeling of identity is established through an uninterrupted series of changes, small and large, whose elaboration and assimilation make it possible to maintain stability and cohesion.

The restrictions imposed by the quarantine unexpectedly opened a crack in that floor on which we walked more or less at ease. It took away rituals, customs, and ways of relating to each other, a social and subjective everyday life that accorded domestic legality to our being in the world. Its impact detonated in very sensitive areas for most of us. The interruption of work routines (with the consequent economic impact), the stillness, the obstacles to free movement and displacement in extra-domestic spaces, the suspension of meeting places (particularly educational ones), the prohibition of contact with the body of others (shaking hands, hugs, kisses), the greeting from a distance, the wearing of masks, the avoidance of objects touched by others or the recurrent washing of hands, clothes, food, and objects that could be potential carriers: a "new normality" was installed in which digital and screen-based communication massively appropriated the intersubjective space as a shelter for bonds, work (the home office), learning and periods of recreation and exchange.

Assimilating the shock and tolerating the uncertainty was necessary to allow active responses from the subjects, and for them to be able to find their way through this predicament. The new routines fulfil the function of sustaining, accompanying, and reencountering our shaken self, as well as providing it with other ways of organizing itself and of moving through the "new normality". Small things, such as doing physical exercise regularly at certain times, taking the dog for a walk, going shopping, taking walks, having virtual chats, taking some new class or course, and watching movies on a regular schedule, are all part of this task.

The time factor has been highlighted as one of the most significant elements in this search for order. The routines derived from concomitant habits (showering, dressing, breakfast, reading or listening to the news, etc.) help to be aware of the passage of time. The home office, the virtual school, and the overlapping moments of leisure led to the experience that time limits have been diluted and to feelings of temporal disorientation. The confinement also generated a slowing down of rhythms and a different experience of temporality, independent of chronology. The beginning and end of the day, the periods of leisure and work, the week and weekend have been associated, in the examples I will cite below, with various rituals that establish marks, organizing, and orienting milestones.

José (40 years old, 2 children) starts the day with a gym session and prepares his favourite coffee. This morning ritual takes the place of the trip he made to school with his children before, moving his body and connecting with it in a different way. Then he has breakfast, reads some news, and gets ready to start working. All this allows him to assimilate the fact of being cooped up all day and to organize the time he spends at home, while he uses in a different way certain moments to which he did not pay attention before. These new routines helped him to overcome the daze and confusion of the first days.

Florencia (35, single) appeals to taking a long nap (the "siesta") during the weekdays and a coffee to welcome the afternoon and prepare for the evening home office. Her friend Pedro finds stimulating a glass of wine or a dance class from 6:30 p.m. on three times a week, or a sports workout twice a week, to mark the end of the workday. These self-imposed activities punctuate the time and accommodate biological rhythms.

Sandra (32, single) and Enrique (35, divorced) set up particular routines to differentiate the week from the weekend, and associate them with different spaces for work and rest. Staying on the balcony sunbathing and listening to musical chords with sounds of nature (sea, wind, birds' trills), watching the stars appear at dusk, and avoiding switching on the computer to work on weekends allow them to continue with their own healthier rhythms. There is another kind of time – a lived, felt one, a time of experience – whose vectors are linked to internal dynamisms, to the vicissitudes and changes of the desiring subject. There have been frequent references to it in psychoanalysis as well as in cinema and literature.

In its conception of neurosis, psychoanalysis often appeals to temporal concepts, as Willy Baranger described: regression, fixation, stages of psychosexual development, transference, repetition, all of which refers to past or present time. Significantly, in the manifestations of psychopathology (neurosis, perversion, characteropathies, psychosis), the temporal dimension of the future disappears. Time also disappears in the schizophrenic, while in the depressive, it stops at the moment of the destruction or loss of the object (time becomes oriented backwards, from the present to the past). Repetition and the repetition compulsion are the basic ways of not accessing the future. That which remains anchored is subtracted from the experience as a whole; it remains outside the psychic circulation and cannot evolve, it is halted in time. We call it a "temporal cleavage", crystallized either in the bodily, the perceptual, the intrapsychic, or the social area. The therapeutic action of interpretation acts retroactively, restoring this crystallized temporal dimension. If we stop to observe the frequent expressions of experiential time during the pandemic, we notice that the abrupt change we had to suffer threw us into uncertainty, waiting, and the impossibility of reorganizing a vital project, all of which translated into modifications in the perception of time that impregnated our subjectivity, reactivating ghosts and latent conflicts in each of us. The sensation of a continuous present, that of a timeless state, the loss of the thread of days or the presence of an indefinite and unstructured time similar to an infinite, that of a dead and overwhelming time or, on the contrary, a distressing and pressing time, are associated and accompanied by feelings of uneasiness, helplessness, catastrophe, and overwhelming disorganization. The wise words that Shakespeare makes Hamlet say in scene V of the first act are fully valid in this context,

"The time is out of joint. O cursed spite,
   That ever I was born to set it right!"

when the ghost of his murdered father summons him to know why the world is unhinged and something smells rotten in Denmark.

Such as Hamlet received the mandate to avenge his father, we are summoned to creatively reinvent our being in the world, integrating the asynchronies, confusions, and hiatuses of an unhinged world in order to continue travelling with ourselves and with others along the paths of this "new time".

This riddle is similar to the one faced by the main character in the 1993 film *The Groundhog Day*, for whom time becomes homogeneous, repetitive, and inevitable, locked as he is in an almost fateful temporal circle. The concept of the "groundhog effect" has been used as a metaphor for personal transformation in order to change course and not become trapped in conditionings and routines, as happens in neuroses and characteropathies. The way out, like the proposal of psychoanalysis, is to bet on desire.

Chaos, uncertainty

These two experiences and ways of dealing with the pandemic have significantly marked the lives of millions of people.

As Ilya Prygogine suggests, "For human beings, to be immutable, to be exempt from change, to have total security and to remain immune to the fickle ups and downs of life, is only feasible when we leave this world, or when we become gods. Horace tells us that the gods are the only beings who lead a risk-free life, exempt from anguish and change".

The idea of chaos, associated with those of evolution, irreversibility, randomness, fluctuations, stochastic processes, is one of the concepts that Prygogine introduced in his revolutionary inclusion of an irreversible temporal arrow in the course of biological and, as we shall see, psychological evolution processes. On the basis of Jacques Monod's statement (in *Chance and Necessity*) that "life is a simple accident in the history of nature", he suggests that the universe in which we live has a plural and complex character: some structures disappear, as in diffusion processes, but others appear, as in biological and, even more clearly, in social processes. Some of these phenomena are adequately described by deterministic equations, but others, such as that of biological evolution, involve stochastic processes.

According to Prygogine, the natural contains essential elements of randomness and irreversibility, as opposed to the artificial, which is deterministic and reversible. This perspective conceives of matter as associated with spontaneous activity, not as something passive, inert. Transitions from chaos to order presuppose and imply the self-organization of matter.

All vital phenomena, including human existence, are inscribed in a complex system that essentially presupposes randomness, unpredictability, and temporal irreversibility. In the field of particles (physical conception), the effect of the absence of equilibrium is to create correlations between these units, that is, to create order from the chaotic movements that originate in the state of equilibrium. Prygogine postulates that order is generated from chaos through non-equilibrium conditions. In a universe where tomorrow is not contained in today, time has to be constructed.

If we try to apply the concepts of the theory of chaos to the functioning of the human psyche, we find that many psychological conceptions, and in particular psychoanalysis, are based on purely deterministic theories. However, the psychic world is a mixture of chance and determinism, since the predictions we make regarding future events are only valid in terms of probabilities. The contribution of Luis Hornstein, who integrates the concepts of the theory of chaos into theoretical and clinical psychoanalytic models, is very interesting. Based on Fechner's theories and in the "principle of constancy", this author finds in the orthodoxy of Freudian metapsychology the knots/axes of the deterministic and reversible vision of psychic functioning. The idea is that an imbalance, provoked by some external (information) or internal (pulsional) stimulus, needs to be suppressed or removed in order to return to the previous point of equilibrium. It is as if man's destiny were only to reduce or neutralize the energy surplus as if he were a closed system.

Freud only had as a theoretical model the thermodynamics of closed systems. Current models present man as an open system tending to disequilibrium, which leads to new re-equilibrations within more complex structures – called "dissipative structures" in Prygogine's chemistry. Let us add that the model of the return to the initial equilibrium leaves no room for chance: everything is determined there. According to Hornstein, "psychoanalysis will be able to advance only if it combines determinism and chance, the algorithmic and the stochastic, the theory of machines and the theory of games". For this author, the unconscious must be considered an open system, and as such capable of self-organization, destructuring, and restructuring; and this is only possible if it is conceived in the context of a "feedback" circuit. Retroaction questions linear causality and supports the very efficacy of analytical work by revealing a form of recursiveness where the present acts on the past, which, however, conditions the significance of the present. Retroaction allows us to think of the advent of the new within the already given.

If we were to consider a linear causality, where the cause produces the effect but the effect does not act on the cause (that is, a unidirectional process), it could be speculated that our present being and feeling were generated by our childhood experiences or our past. By including the idea of retroaction, we open the door to consider that also the present or current influences the past. In fact, analytical work makes it possible to re-signify the past, to destructure it in order to allow a restructuring. In this instance, the re-signified past would act effectively and operatively as a driving force to achieve changes in our present behaviour.

If we review the vicissitudes of the therapeutic processes from this point of view, we will see that resistance to change, to not modifying anything, requires less energy than those processes which demand change. It can be assumed that an important amount of energy is spent in the resolution of the internal conflict and in the defensive support necessary to counterbalance the anguish that would be provoked by the release of drives. When the individual is unstructured (chaos, disorder) and must choose between returning to the previous scheme and seeking new paths (a bifurcation point), he/she is extremely sensitive to the influence of the external environment, particularly to the analyst's word. Chance circumstances occurring in that context and at that time will have very important effects. This will enhance the formation of a new order, a new structure oriented towards the cure.

All this leads us to conceive the psyche as a joint product of determinism and chance. That is why human behaviour is not wholly predictable. And, following Prygogine, we could consider chance as something that is an objective part of reality.

The present pandemic has been offering us very varied and enriching examples of all of the above. Undoubtedly, the appearance of the pandemic had a disruptive effect worldwide. It produced destabilization, disorganization, and also chaos in the lives and routines of millions of people, who suddenly saw their way of being in the world interrupted and altered. The random and unpredictable were installed in such a way that the temporal arrow marked an undeniable irreversibility between what was before and what would come after. In addition to the mass phenomena discussed above, individuals, families, and societies can be understood as part of complex systems or structures, exposed to processes of chaos, restructuring, or spontaneous self-organization. The initial responses of fear, astonishment, and helplessness were followed by denial, rebellion, and uncertainty.

Being able to settle into the "new normality" meant not only assimilating the innumerable restrictions derived from care (control, prevention of contagion) but also, and essentially, going through the mourning of greater or lesser intensity that accompanied this process. The death of loved ones (relatives, friends), varying degrees of disability and post-illness physical and psychological sequels, economic and labour damages (closed businesses, loss of source of employment, loss of clients) in areas such as tourism, gastronomy, entertainment, services, etc., restrictions on contact with others, the impossibility of seeing each other in full (bare face), of touching, hugging, meeting in groups, moving around and wandering freely, brought isolation, loneliness, and depression. Those who resisted/resist the changes were caught by the fear of present and future catastrophe, by the frustrating sensation of lost time, of a too long pause imposed on their lives.

But those who assimilated and processed the impacts saw and faced new possibilities and ways of leaving behind the crossroads in which they found themselves. This led to finding new and unknown tools and alternatives, in this novel learning and reality transformation process with which they had to deal. This bifurcation point gave rise to an unexpected and previously unpredictable organization in fields such as education, health, science and technology, and bonding.

In a February 2021 article, *The Economist* made predictions about several areas of future life that illustrate these ongoing changes and transformations of the "new normality":

1   Humans want to socialize again, but the home office will basically stay the same. The mixed model of work is unrealistic; we will simply continue to work online from our homes, increasingly adapted to it, and meeting in different places each month to make fun, socialize and connect. Multiple spaces will be created to hold large digital board meetings that may solve everything. No one will want to bear the city traffic or to be trapped again in the maelstrom of information and work.

2   Offices are closing in a very high percentage and this backward model is taken over by disruptive technologies. Every day we will have more digital assistants to work efficiently. Large corporations will be remembered forever as the huge mammoths of 1980–2020 in extinction. People did not always work that way and will not work that way forever.

3   "Work hotels" will disappear by at least 50%. Business travel, congresses, or meetings will cease to be what they were, if work can be done online. Business tourism will practically disappear. Calls will become video calls, international meetings will be done online, well-attended congresses will turn into technological systems. There will be new products launched in digital form and new technologies. Congresses will be supported by artificial intelligence (AI) so that people can have personal experiences.

4   Homes will incorporate more technological items better adapted to daily work. Many companies will be dedicated to solving the problems created by home working. The very concept of "home" will change. Today one can live outside a big city, work the same than before and generate the same value. Physical location will be a priority for companies, but a secondary issue for workers.

5   Productivity will no longer depend on a boss who reviews the operators, but on platforms that help measure results, key performance indicators (KPIs), and efficient times. The way to hire personnel will be rethought. Today, hiring the best worker in the world in any area is easier, cheaper, and more effective than before. There will be no difference between hiring local and foreign personnel. Today we are all global.

6   All places to which people go frequently (churches, art shows, gyms, cinemas, shows) become virtual and conform to the subscription scheme. Sometimes physical events will be attended, but the numbers will not be enough to maintain the previous physical infrastructures. Fewer places will be able to keep open several alternatives. Very soon, there will be sophisticated services delivered at home through virtual reality.

7 Companies that do not invest at least 10% of their capital in new technologies will disappear. In 2020, the traditional company will come to an end: we can only wait for its definitive death. With limited resources, companies require more certainty and better investments. A new and innovative technology company can now replace one that has been doing the same thing for the last fifty years. Many services will copy the booming "dark kitchen" model.

8 Entertainment tourism will return fully strengthened in the second half of 2021, always accompanied by a lot of technology in all its stages, from the purchase, the operation and the experiences it will allow. People will appreciate more than ever to visit natural places but with highly technological resources. They will go to more remote spots and will want to live more authentic experiences supported with digital assistance at all times. Interaction will be the basis of future entertainment. People will want to be part of it, to experience something authentic and to discover information dynamically.

9 The handling of personal data will become more sensitive and large platforms will change. People will prefer to pay for subscription services because of their greater transparency: they will rather pay than give away their data. Currently, big brands are worth their credibility. Everything can be copied or replicated, except prestige. Nowadays, the value of a company depends on many factors and not only on its annual sales.

10 The workforce will be significantly reduced and many simple operations will be assigned to AI. By 2024, AI will be already handling complicated operations in millions of locations. But widespread adoption will begin in 2021. A very extensive season of global layoffs is coming. Unemployment will ensue for multiple reasons and not just because of the economic crisis.

11 Education will never be what it was: it will become face-to-face but technologically adaptive. Everyone will be given what he/she needs. Studying offline and online will be the norm. Schools and universities will adopt a hybrid scheme forever. Highly qualified people will continue to be hired for important positions, but for less important ones, candidates without a university degree, who have the necessary experience, will be accepted.

12 The medical system has adapted to the digital world with remote technology forever. A teleconference medical appointment will be the norm. People will continue with rapid Covid testing throughout 2021 to feel safe. Vaccine procurement will be greatly accelerated but will face significant challenges along the way. Large hospitals will have to rethink their way of operating because of the financial crisis they have suffered in the wake of COVID 19. Thanks to permanent personal hygiene, people will get sick less frequently from viruses, bacteria, and the ailments that depend on poor food handling.

13 The personal economy will contract, new ways of generating business transactions will be created and people will save more. A high percentage of household spending will go to activities that were previously free, and vice versa. Certain items, such as elegant clothes, will be replaced by casual garments. A radical transformation of habits began in 2021. Electronic items will continue to be the most appreciated and purchased products for another year.

14 Commerce will continue to grow, but in virtual form; new players, such as Facebook, TikTok, and YouTube, will compete with Amazon. Around 50% of local stores will close worldwide. Those that provide personal experiences and showrooms will survive, but by the end of 2024, commerce will be greater online than in person in many areas. Large shopping malls will be trapped in time: very few will survive in the long term.

15 Climate change will be a hotly debated topic. Large industries will transform themselves thanks to AI for a better understanding of their operations and functioning. As a result of the transformation of cities, the adoption of the bicycle as a primary mode of transportation will continue to increase. There will be a natural shift from Covid to climate change as the main topic of discussion. Countries will have an opportunity to come together to help solve major common problems.

16 New subscription-based news and information models, endowed with greater transparency, will help to disseminate content without so many "fake news". Credibility and transparency will be the cornerstones of all companies. Tired of the flood of information, people will prefer to interact in systems coordinated by experts. Immediacy will continue to be highly valued.

17 Mental health will become a recurring problem and large platforms will help people to cope with the aggression, loneliness, and anguish they have experienced in isolation. One of the big liabilities 2020 will leave behind is the complication of working as a team again. There will be much to discuss, much to rethink. Leadership crises in companies will become more common every day.

18 The great problems of nations, such as education, health, energy, security, politics, the destruction of the middle class, will come to the forefront and technology companies will offer solutions for them. Huge amounts of capital will be invested in social welfare, while some global obstacles will be solved. Social entrepreneurship will reach its peak, with substantially good economic results.

19 Everything (food, personal experiences, and ways of interacting) will aim to be natural and healthy. The present way of life will be 100% natural. Producing one's own food, meditating, and practicing physical exercise will be part of every day. Permaculture and efficient production systems personally managed will grow exponentially. Everyone will

want to satisfy their food needs in a healthy and personal way, consuming "local but real". Being healthier will be the "new luxury". Fancy products will lose any justification and value. After a year of uncontrollable waste, recycling will come back more strongly, with new technologies that effectively solve the problems it had generated in the past.
20   The world expects the year 2021 to be a new beginning, a rebirth. People will rethink their personal, work, health, money, and spiritual goals. There will be great opportunities to satisfy all these requirements, and changes in the way of thinking. There will indeed be a new beginning, with more real values. Many behaviours will be transformed and some will never return. Hoarding, consuming in excess, and living to achieve material well-being only will be on the negative side of the equation.

So much for *The Economist*. Innovations, technology, a more natural way of living, and lateral thinking are the basis of this new reality. In 2021, to continue doing the same thing as before without reconsider anything is to go ahead straight to the precipice. There is still time for everyone to find a new path. The guidelines are defined. It is simply a matter of finding new routes, either in personal matters or in business activities.

Uncertainty

Another major effect of this pandemic is the experience of uncertainty. We have been plunged into a situation that causes us "the lack of a certain and reliable knowledge about what is happening" and what will happen to us. Its opposite, certainty, is the result of a clear, reliable, and sure knowledge of things, or of the absence of doubt. It allows us to adhere to something knowable without fear of making mistakes, of failing.

Uncertainty evokes and reactivates early experiences of helplessness, with its correlate of anguish, distress, and confusion. Depending on its intensity and duration, it may lead to states of suffering and psychic disorganization.

Throughout its cultural evolution, humanity has known how to compensate the distressing effects that it had provoked and how to defend itself, both individually and collectively. At the cost of important instinctual renunciations, it has built the edifice of culture, which provides "the knowledge and power conquered by men to dominate the forces of nature" (Freud, "The Future of an Illusion", 1927).

Likewise, since ancient times individuals have deposited in magic and religions the illusion and belief in powerful protective figures, parental substitutes that would protect them from the onslaught of the forces of Nature, which continuously confront them, in a cruel and inexorable way, with the reality of their feeble existence.

At present, the absence of conclusive answers, on both the spiritual and cultural planes, from the sciences in spite of the power of their knowledge also injures our narcissism and our ideals, increasing our anxious fear and sense of perplexity.

The stamp of uncertainty becomes starker as doubts and the absence of certainties spread. Doubts about how long this situation will persist, how much immunity we will have if we become infected to protect us from a relapse or a new infection, how effective and long-lasting are the experimental vaccines being applied, and what harmful side effects they may have in the medium and long term. Or how many strains or mutations of COVID, perhaps more lethal than the current ones, are active. Today the sources of suffering extend to:

- The threatening active presence of the virus and its association with the idea of death (one's own death or that of loved ones). Since the beginning of the pandemic, this association has been sustained and repeated incessantly by images, audios, publications, and speeches broadcast by the media.
- Fear of contagion and of being hospitalized, intubated on a respirator, or of being confined or isolated and perhaps socially segregated for a prolonged period of time.
- Deprivation and restriction to carry out actions and exchanges in subjectivizing contexts. Subjects normally deposit aspects of themselves in these contexts, and their identity, self-esteem, and internal cohesion are sustained by them. They operate as important organizers and structuring agents of psychic life.
- The primary ties with family and friends, the exercise of work activities for adults and educational activities for children and young people, and to a lesser extent, the possibility of sharing spaces for physical, sports, recreational, and cultural activities.
- Economic difficulties.
- The disruption of time.

Janine Puget highlights the feeling of perplexity as a conscious manifestation of the so-called "uncertainty principle". She states that the unpredictable, with all its vicissitudes, may give rise to a valid suffering, just as chaos responds to a logic of complexity.

In order to endure the alternatives of everyday life, subjects need to sustain, in an illusory way, their need for certainty, truth, and knowledge. To be able to think themselves on stable, coherent, and predictable bases, a defence is established that protects them from the intrusion of "the alien", with its correlate of unpredictability and randomness. There is a critical point marked by the possibility of continuing to recognize oneself as belonging to a determined space and time within a bonding organization.

Conscious and unconscious memories allow tolerating the novelty within variable levels or margins for each subject. In such a case, the illusion of certainty and predictability can disappear and be replaced by another without excessively dramatic consequences and without generating disorganization and pain. If the structural and defensive rigidity is greater, states of anguish appear that lead to disorientation, confusion, and panic.

Puget's emphasis is on bonding and the fact that unpredictable events occur regularly, as if they were a structural condition. Subjects need to sustain the "protective" illusion of predictability through their adhesion or membership in social groups on the basis of custom, of what they have already lived. To do so, they must leave out or stop those experiences that contradict that illusion almost on a daily basis. According to Puget, bonds, which she conceives as belonging to the intersubjective and transubjective space, originate actions in an absolutely unpredictable way. Such actions do not depend on variables that can be understood, but are only the consequence of a certain type of connectivity.

Are there ways to protect oneself against uncertainty or to attenuate its effects?

Baruch Spinoza writes in his *Ethics* about hope and defines it as "an unceasing joy, springing from the idea of a future or past thing, the effectiveness of which we somehow doubt", and defines fear as "an inconstant sadness". According to his philosophy, the passions of fear and hope make it possible to understand various religious, political, and ethical problems. Fear is, for him, the enemy of reason and he declares that hope justifies waiting for a saviour, which promotes resignation and obedience. Spinoza affirms that fear and hope dominate imagination and uncertainty, transforming the subject into a passive being at the service of power. He maintains the need for an active hope, which would allow "an immanent search to find the joy of what is necessary in the potency of being".

In our days, maintaining hope is not only an act of faith but could be articulated with a set of intra and transubjective processes that allow to transform perplexity and suffering into pragmatic actions and responses. The capacity to tolerate the uncertain, together with the acceptance of what has been lost and perhaps will not be found again (mourning), can open the way to connect with others and experience new modalities, modified routines, and unexplored options.

We must resort to reassuring memories of past experiences in which the crisis was confronted and successfully overcome, sustained, and accompanied by the affective and erogenous bonding of our group and by our social belongings, which form a supporting network in the face of the uncertain and distressing.

Bibliography

Agamben, G. (2021) *Where are we now, the epidemic as politics.* London: Eris.
Arendt, H. (2003) *The origins of totalitarism.* UK: Mariner Books.

Baranger, W. (1962) 'La dimension temporal del conflicto', *Revista Uruguaya de Psicoanálisis*, 4.

BBC News website, Paul, R. (March 15, 2018). Stephen Hawking's warnings: What he predicted for the future. https://www.bbc.com/news/science-environment-43408961

Foucault, M. (1991) *Microphysics of power in discipline and punishment*. New York: Vintage Books.

Freud, S. (1921) *Group psychology and analysis of the Ego*, standard ed., vol XVIII.

Freud, S. (1927) *The future of an Illusion*, standard ed., vol XXI.

Grinberg, L. (1990) *The goals of psychoanalysis, Identification, identity and supervision*. London: Karnac Books.

Hornstein, L (1999) Temporalidad. Determinación, azar. Lo reversible y lo irreversible, en Revista Internacional de Psicoanalisis Aperturas, numero 2. 1999.

Kaes, R. (1994) 'Psychic work and unconscious alliances in therapeutic institutions', *British Journal of Psychotherapy*, 10(3).

Machiavelli, N. (2016) *The Prince*. UK: Routledge.

Milgram, S. (1974) *Obedience to Authority and Experimental View*. New York: Harper Perennial.

Prigogyne, I. (1983) *Only an Illusion*. Utah University.

Prigogyne, I. (2018) *The end of certainty, time, chaos and the new laws of nature*. New York: The Free Press.

Puget, J. (2015) *Subjetivación discontinua y psicoanálisis, Incertidumbre y certezas*. Buenos Aires: Lugar Editorial.

Schmitt, C. (2016) *The Oxford handbook of Carl Schmitt*. New York: Harvard University Press.

Shakespeare, W. (1899) *The tragedy of Hamlet*, edited by Edward Dowden. London: Methuen and Co.

Spinoza Baruch, (1996) *Routledge Philosophy Guidebook to Spinoza and the Ethics*, By Genevieve Lloyd.

The Economist http://miningpress.com/nota/335247/the-economist-2021-y-virus-segun-50-expertos

Zizek, S. (2020) *Pandemic, Covid 19 shakes the world*. New York: Polity Press.

Conclusion

In these pages, we examine the psychological processes and manifestations of various events in our cultural, social, and biological environment that have left their mark or imprint on our psyche. Since the pandemic and the appropriation, invasion, and generalization of new technologies, there have been numerous changes and true revolutions in our daily lives. They accentuated many of the codes and values we shared in postmodernism, such as globalization, market rules, and the tendency to speed and efficiency.

One of the vassals of our Ego is that which comes from the external reality, the environment, the media, the links with others, the culture, and its ideals. They affect how individuals feel as long as they can integrate and accommodate themselves to these conditions, which in turn have repercussions on their being, on the constitution of their subjectivity.

Understanding the new normality and processing its codes is the test, challenge, or trauma ahead of us. The new normality includes postmodern cultural values and ideals already incorporated into our societies, the changes introduced by new technologies, and the experiences we have been going through with the pandemic.

Things are done in a different way, people live differently, and other elements become relevant. Machines began to compete in time, trustworthiness, and quality of stimuli with humans, offering models with new codes to representational structures. However, the diminished human-object contact, the lack of its unique and special imprint, exposes us to have few non-traumatic thresholds. At the same time, it is necessary to dedicate some time to a satisfactory object presence in order to appropriate the stimuli and initiate the processes of symbolization, to assimilate the external offer to the Ego, to identify and not generate an overadaptation or an adhesive identification with what is exhibited on the screens.

Verbalization gives way to visualization. The subject is replaced by the user. Although symbols and cultural references are established, the trend to modify communications with a predominance of signs prevails. And these signs lose their referential charge in a space without history and without territory. We are tempted to look for universal and massive models and to

DOI: 10.4324/9781003293569-7

lose the modesty and intimacy of private spaces, which have become public. Language and the system of meanings were modified, which brought with it the appearance of other modes of transmission and learning, different ways of being informed and of positioning oneself in the face of the unknown.

The communicational shift brought about new ways of establishing links and behaving, virtual encounters, and virtual ways of finding partners, friends, followers, and adherents. Everyone can be hidden or visible, participate or spy, with the magic of a "click on" or a "click off". These bonding conditions, which restricted bodily presence, were greatly accentuated during the pandemic and facilitated the creation of new routines for work, meetings, and interpersonal contacts in general. They became a means of creating subjective spaces in the face of the fears and uncertainties that affected, among other things, sensoriality and the perception of time. Communication devices such as mobile phones were gradually transformed into a source of security and companionship due to the multiplicity of areas they have occupied, including the hours dedicated to work, exchange or transfer of goods, etc. During the peak period of the pandemic, with physical separateness established to prevent contagion, they were a lifeline and a way to be connected for many people.

In social terms, subjectivity suffers the ups and downs of political, climatic, biological, and technological events which affect it. All these events have random and often unpredictable variations. They lead to situations of uncertainty, generate overlaps, discontinuities, and heterologies. The belonging, continuity, and sustainability of human relations depend on the groups and masses in which individuals come together and on the pacts they establish, which take into account the new modes of bonding and integration. Chaos and chance will go hand in hand with the conception of a psyche and an unconscious open to exchanges with the outside, with the surrounding environment, allowing the former to disorganize and reorganize itself in order to create, from new events and experiences, novel forms and models of identification.

We are necessarily exposed to de-structuring and de-subjectivizing moments that force us to reconstitute and resignify our own subjectivity. Subjects are no longer only an origin that includes their Oedipal conflicts and transgenerational memories, but a becoming that alters their identity, transfixed by events and situations that leave their mark on them.

The aforementioned set of changes had a traumatic effect on the minds and bodies of individuals, groups, and societies. To assimilate the traumas, to attempt their symbolic elaboration and to mourn for what has been lost is a fundamental and crucial task for our subjective constitution. We are who we are because we have left behind the obstacles that were in our way. As a response to traumas, mourning seeks to reestablish the cohesion and stability of the Ego that has been shaken and affected by the surprising or foreseeable impact. We will not be the same after it. We come out of this process with a trail of scars, of marks that signal our journey through life. These experiences, which have left their mark on us, imply a turn, a change of axis that forces us to give up the position in which we found ourselves. In this flow, the old lost identity slips away; it is a desubjectivation process that alters our sense of ourselves until we meet with a new subjectivity.

When we are unable to elaborate the many traumatic episodes and do not manage to consolidate the shreds of ourselves that remain along the way, we find ourselves with clinical pictures of our days, such as panic and fanaticism in their current clothes, which highlight the effects of anguish, disorganization, and identificatory and structural emptiness, resulting from an outside attack on previously fragilized organizations.

The feeling of self can also be challenged and drive many subjects to search for in nature adventures and sensations of purity, freedom, and energetic resurgence to counteract emptiness, oppression, or hopelessness. The biological pleasure by the release of stimulating endogenous amines, and the narcissistic massage to the own Ego that they receive, offered as an object of social consumption, is also widely observed in the twists and turns that the digital world and the virtual networks offerthrough connection, entertainment, contacts and "likes".

The new normality we are going through has modified the times of life and forced us to change routines, to coexist with uncertainty, and to learn other languages and ways of behaviour. It means that before or after the elaboration of traumas and mourning, we will have to meet again with our subjectivities in the roads to come.

Index

For Product Safety Concerns and Information please contact our EU
representative GPSR@taylorandfrancis.com
Taylor & Francis Verlag GmbH, Kaufingerstraße 24, 80331 München, Germany

9 781032 276328